"LET BROTHERLY LOVE CONTINUE"

THE

*L*OVE

REVOLUTION

♡

*d*s DESIGN SOLUTIONS ®

EASTWOOD ANABA

"LET BROTHERLY LOVE CONTINUE"

THE LOVE REVOLUTION

Unless otherwise indicated, all scripture quotations in this book are from
the King James Version of the Bible (KJV)

ISBN 978-9988-0-9858-8

Request for information should be addressed to
The Administrator
Desert Leaf Publications
P. O. Box 299
Bolgatanga, UER, Ghana, W/A
Tel: +233-72 23077
E-mail: eastperl@africaonline.com.gh
         fgc@africaonline.com.gh
Website: www.eastwoodanaba.com
www.fountaingatechapel.org

Design & Production
DESIGN SOLUTIONS
Tel: +233-21 810410
      +233-20 8150930
      +233-20 8231223
E-mail: georgepabi@yahoo.com
afuapabi@yahoo.com

Printed in Gt Britain By Polestar Group

CONTENTS

INTRODUCTION

*L*ove is the most potent force in the universe. It is the spirit behind *every virtue and the life of every spiritual gift*. **There can be no eternal life without eternal love.** Eternal death is the result of a lack of eternal love. Eternal death set in because of disobedience in the Garden of Eden. Jesus said that if we loved Him we would keep His commandments. If Adam and Eve's love for God were perfect they would never have disobeyed God. They disobeyed because they did not walk in perfect love. Without love we die prematurely. If we walk in perfect love, God will not judge us and sentence us to death. I believe that the Church must address the issue of the lack of love. We must know what the true love of God is and yield to the Holy Spirit for this love to flow through us.

Selfishness has seized the soul of the Church, with thousands of believers completely indifferent about what happens to others.

We would give to one another if we loved enough.

We shall die for one another if we love enough.

A world saturated with love cannot be plunged into a state of chaos.

Love is more important than any other thing. Stop pursuing the things you are pursuing and start loving.

Love is the force of heaven that ejected the Lord Jesus from the Father's bosom to come and save us. Love is the factor that moved deity to clothe Himself in human flesh in order to save lost humanity. God is love. Religion without love is void of the life of God. Love is the breath and life of every spiritual virtue – there can be no patience, holiness, self-control, meekness or godliness without love.

The love that distils out of the heart of the Father is pure and selfless. The whole world is unanimous in the knowledge that love is a needed ingredient. Love in its pure form is the most potent force through which God expresses Himself to mankind. It would have been great if the love of God that operates amongst people were in the same pure form in which it occurs in the heart of the Father. Unfortunately, the version of love that we have is mostly pretentious and selfish. Even the Church of our time is struggling to discover and practise the God kind of love.

The preacher's heart is yet to grasp the love in the gospel he is professionally dispensing. The church member is perplexed by the yawning gap between the life of Christ and the lives of the numerous worshippers who flood our churches Sunday after Sunday. Wrong motives, greed, fear and selfish ambition have combined to deny true love any expression in the Church. Jesus warned that in the last days the love of many shall wax cold – love would be frozen and cannot flow amongst us.

The manifestation of this coldness of love is very clear. There are rumours of war. Nations are rising against nations and kingdoms are at daggers drawn with one another. The beginning of sorrows has caught up with us. Believers are delivered to be afflicted all over the world. They are killed and hated by those that hate the name of Jesus. As Jesus predicted offences have multiplied with the concomitants of the betrayal of one another and hatred. False prophets are on the rampage, unleashing the deadly poison of deception on their prey. Love does not motivate the apostles of error but personal gain does. The words of Jesus are so true – iniquity has abounded.

This book is timely intervention for the modern day Church which I can liken to the Laodicean Church of the book of Revelation. This Church is the worldly Church. It is neither cold nor hot – it is lukewarm in its love towards Jesus and the saints. Jesus rebuked the Church and commanded it to repent.

> *And unto the angel of the church of the Laodiceans write; These things saith the Amen, the faithful and true witness, the beginning of the creation of God;*
>
> *I know thy works, that thou art neither cold nor hot: I would thou wert cold or hot.*
>
> *So then because thou art lukewarm, and neither cold nor hot, I will spue thee out of my mouth.*
>
> *Because thou sayest, I am rich, and increased with goods, and have need of nothing; and knowest not that thou art wretched, and miserable, and poor, and blind, and naked:*
>
> *I counsel thee to buy of me gold tried in the fire, that thou mayest be rich; and white raiment, that thou mayest be clothed, and that the shame of thy nakedness do not appear; and anoint thine eyes with eyesalve, that thou mayest see.*
>
> *As many as I love, I rebuke and chasten: be zealous therefore, and repent.*
>
> *Behold, I stand at the door, and knock: if any man hear my voice, and open the door, I will come in to him, and will sup with him, and he with me.*

> *To him that overcometh will I grant to sit with me in my throne, even as I also overcame, and am set down with my Father in his throne.*
>
> *He that hath an ear, let him hear what the Spirit saith unto the churches.*
>
> Revelation 3:14-22

The Laodicean Church prided itself in the wrong things. It was very boastful and for the wrong reasons. This backslidden assembly boasted in riches and the accumulation of goods. Steeped in their warped philosophy of life, they did not know that they were wretched, miserable, poor, blind and naked. Talk to most charismatic Christians and you would see immediately that the Laodicean Church is in our midst. The airwaves and streets of most cities that have churches are choked with the worldly emphasis of preachers who have departed from the Word of God.

We are pursuing riches and success at the expense of our souls. The swelling of the numbers of congregants in churches is seriously being confused with the approval of God and the evidence of His presence. I am afraid that worldly standards have displaced true godliness in many hearts. When success is everything we are in trouble. Churches which replace God with gold, love with lust and the presence of God with shameless pretence, are gaining prominence everywhere. The true worshippers of God cannot be seen. Indeed the true lights have been placed under bushels by worldly Christians who would do anything to empower those that tickle them and satisfy their carnal instincts.

The condition of the Church calls for a revolution. Like the Laodicean Church we are lukewarm. We are neither hot nor cold. The lyrics of our songs are not clear and it is difficult to tell whether our sermons are inspired by heaven or hell. The words of Jesus to the Church of Ephesus, which urged them to return to their first love is appropriate for our generation (Revelation 2:3). Just like the Laodiceans, the Ephesians had deteriorated in the quality of their worship. I hear the voice of the Lord similarly calling the Church of today to repentance – we must return to our first love.

THE ABSENCE OF LOVE IN THE CHURCH CALLS FOR A REVOLUTION. A REVOLUTION CAN BE DEFINED AS A SUDDEN AND DRASTIC CHANGE. IT IS A SUDDEN TURN AROUND.

When I consider the rate at which love is being removed from the Church and society as a whole, I have a feeling that we need a LOVE REVOLUTION. Love must be rushed back into the Church and this must be done now. We must use every radical means within scriptural standards to restore love to the Church.

We must change our priorities in the Body of Christ. The pursuit of success, prosperity and breakthroughs should not drive us to betray one another just to achieve our goals. It is time for radical heart searching. We cannot continue to divide the body of Christ with doctrines and attitudes that are aimed at making us happy and fulfilled at the expense of everybody else.

Churches are splitting all around us. Families are plagued with suspicion and mistrust. Children find more solace in the arms of strange friends and thugs than in the homes of their own parents. The greatest of all virtues is love. Sadly, this panacea of all human problems has been relegated to the background. We are heading for disaster. There must be a sudden and radical turn around to restore love to the body of Christ. Let us get the love revolution underway.

CHAPTER 1

UNDERSTANDING THE LOVE OF GOD

*P*aul prayed for the Ephesians to be able to comprehend the breadth, length, depth and height of the love of God. The above dimensions are more than one needs to calculate volume (length x breadth x height) or area (length x breadth). This means that the love of God cannot be measured. We cannot talk about its area or its volume. It is impossible to fully comprehend the love of God.

> *May be able to comprehend with all saints what is the breadth, and length, and depth, and height;*
>   *And to know the love of Christ, which passeth knowledge, that ye might be filled with all the fulness of God.*
>
> *Ephesians 3:18-19*

The love of God in the above verse is *agapao* which is usually referred to as the God kind of love. It is **unconditional love** that flows towards even our enemies. It is different from phileo love which is the love we show towards our friends and loved ones. God loved us even while we were sinners. Agape love flows towards its recipients even if they are not giving anything back.

Agape love does not wait for others to come to it. It rather reaches out to them. The Lord showed me something about forgiveness a short while ago. We often wait for those who wrong us to come to us and confess their sins and repent before we forgive them. The Lord taught me otherwise.

If we allow people to come and kneel down and humiliate themselves before us, before we forgive them, we have no reward in heaven. The humiliated person earns his forgiveness with his humility and we have our reward on earth, because he made us feel good. With the God kind of love, Christ died for us while we were yet sinners.

There should be a passionate desire in the heart of every believer to know and appreciate the love of God. We cannot live a fulfilling life in God without understanding the love of God. The depth of our knowledge of the love of God determines our ability to walk in His ways and manifest His glory.

The breadth of the love of God speaks about **the reach of God's love**. He reached out from heaven and delivered us from sin and death. God reached downwards from deity to humanity to save us. Jesus was made flesh to take our place in death. **The length** of the love of God refers to **the longsuffering of God's love**. He is patient to the last minute. God is not swift to judge and destroy the sinner. The patience of Jesus made Him go as far as to the cross to save us. **The depth** of eternal love refers to the **lowest realms of the grave and the power of death, the grave and hades.** Jesus sank in order to lift the sinner out. He took our place in death. God took us out of the horrible pit of hell and set our feet on the rock. Finally **the height** of the love of God points to **the exalted realm** this love raises us to. God has elevated us to sit together in Christ in heavenly places.

The way of love is no easy route. Love is very demanding and we can only walk in love if we follow the example of Jesus. It is impossible to walk in love without the Spirit of Christ.

Paul makes it clear in the scripture verses above that the love of Christ passes knowledge. The New Living Translation of the Bible says that it is so great that you will never fully understand it. The Living Bible says that it is so great that you will never see the end of it or fully know and understand it.

The love of God is past knowledge– it cannot be understood. In this chapter we wish to understand the love of God. How can we understand something that cannot be understood?

What we should understand about the love of God is that it cannot be understood. Love is not a logical thing. It does not make sense. It flows unrestrained in the human heart only after God has transformed the heart. Love cannot be captured in the structured and configured reasoning of the intellect. Love is not a mind thing but a heart thing.

The Initiative Of Love

Love does not wait to be approached; it takes the initiative to find people. When we all look behind us we shall see the footprints of the love of God. The footprints of love are the wonderful deeds of God towards us in the past. We love Him because He first loved us. While we were yet sinners Christ died for us. God loved us when we had done everything wrong. His love is not determined by the things we do or don't do.

> *We love him, because he first loved us.*
> 1 John 4:19

Love does not wait to be approached – it takes the first step forward. This explains why the gospel of Jesus Christ is a "go ye

therefore gospel" and not a "wait for them to come gospel".

We must not wait for the sinner to come to us. We must go to them. Jesus did not wait for us to come to Him but He rather came to us. The habit of waiting for people to come to us and to love us first is killing every holy institution and fellowship amongst us. Marriages are suffering because both husband and wife have the sickness of waiting to be loved first. Churches are breaking up because everybody wants attention.

I had a very memorable experience with a spiritual father of mine, Rev. Peter Awindor in Bolgatanga on the 25th September 2006. I passed by my office to say goodbye to my executive assistant on my way to a speaking appointment in Accra. As soon as I entered his office Rev. Awindor came in. For some months my wife had been urging us to visit him at his home but I could not make the time to do so. When the man of God entered the office I thought he was going to rebuke me and accuse me of not visiting him. I began to apologise to him immediately and confess my sin of negligence.

Instead of rebuking me he rather commended me for the work the Lord was doing through me in the Northern part of Ghana and around the world. He also thanked me for the love I showed him from time to time. After encouraging me awhile he took hold of my hand to pray for me. I knelt down immediately and received the blessing and prayer of this apostle of God. After that I apologised to him again for not coming home for some time because of my busy schedule. I received peace in my heart and embarked on a successful journey. I learned later on that my big sister and mother had had some terrible dreams about a bad event occurring in the family. Before the trip of that day I had no peace in my heart but after the prayer of Rev. Awindor peace overwhelmed my heart. I believe that God sent the man of God to bless me and release me from something I had no idea about.

Rev. Awindor came to give love and not to receive it. It is more blessed to give than to receive. I meet people who when they see me don't even ask how I am doing before they begin to accuse me of not looking for them. Too many people believe that it is their right to receive attention from everybody. God loved us first. He did not wait for us to love Him first.

Nobody is ready to die for another person. We have distorted the scriptural revelation that we should love our neighbour as ourselves. It is easy to think that we should love our neighbour as ourselves but not more than ourselves. Let us look at this a little bit. The peak of your love for yourself is that you are ready to die for yourself. If you know that the only way you can please God or achieve a great objective is to die you will be ready to do so. In the same way if we love our neighbours as ourselves we shall be ready to lay down our lives for one another. To love your neighbour as yourself will ultimately mean that you have to love your neighbour more than yourself.

> *Hereby perceive we the love of God, because he laid down his life for us: and we ought to lay down our lives for the brethren.*
>
> *1 John 3:16*

To lay down our lives for one another would mean that we have to die whilst they are alive. This would mean loving your neighbor more than yourself. Does this contradict loving your neighbor as yourself? No. The truth is that we would all love if someone laid down his life for us. What Jesus was saying was that just as you would love others to lay down their lives for you, you must also be ready to lay down your life for someone else.

Hereby perceive we the love of God – He laid down His life for us. Many marriages and ministries lack this heavenly philosophy. Selfishness has seized the souls of several institutions of men and greed has generated conflicts in relationships that were meant for mutual blessing. Our generation has specialized in forging marriages of convenience and establishing alliances that thrive on the spirit of commensalism. Exchange is our language and not giving.

We are withholding so much from one another that nobody is truly living. One can only truly live if another person is ready to die. We could not have lived spiritually if Jesus had not died.

Recently I had a meeting with a young man who wanted attention from everybody but was not ready to give attention to anybody. He complained, whined and moaned about everything and everybody. His position was that nobody loved him. Nobody cared. This attitude of self-pity is a manifestation of a lack of divine love in a person's heart. A lady jumped out of a prayer meeting in our church and caught up with my wife around the church premises and vowed never to forgive some young ladies who had offended her in the church. She wanted attention. Some brethren had judged a matter between her daughter and other people and she was not satisfied because things did not go her way. She wanted my wife to give a counter judgement. We realised later on that she had been harbouring bitterness in her heart against the people for years. Such is the attitude of our self-seeking generation.

The love of God is not logical. It led Jesus to die in the place of sinners. He who knew no sin died for sinners. He was wounded for our transgressions and bruised for our iniquities. This is not logical – the sinless died for the sinful. How do you feel when people shirk their responsibilities and you have to do it? When your husband fails to provide for the home and as a wife you have to do it, it can be painful. Yet this is how your love is tested.

Love would move you to do things for people, which they cannot do for themselves. Others would squander their lives and resources and fall back on you for help and sometimes you have no choice but to help them. As a pastor I have seen many cases where people waste their lives and refuse to pay the price to walk in wise counsel. They insist on their paths of rebellion. However, when it is time to reap the consequences of their actions, they come to me for help. Though painful, the love of God moves me to assist people like this over and over again. The father of the prodigal son in the Bible received him after he had messed his life up. There are times I have refused to help such erring people just to compel them to be responsible.

The love of God draws people. Jesus said that they that come to Him, He would in no wise cast out. He came to us and we responded by going to Him. His love drew us. He did not only draw us to Himself but He shared His life, His kingdom and even His Father with us. This love passes human knowledge. It cannot be contained in a human heart unless the heart is born again. Naturally, we cannot walk in real love without destroying ourselves. This love will kill us if we attempt to practise it in the flesh. It must be generated by the Holy Spirit in us and released by His power through us. If an electrical appliance is meant to be operated with 110-volt electrical power and you plug it into a 220-volt power source it would blow up, if you switched it on.

The love of God will blow a human heart up if it flows through it. Something must happen to our hearts before the love of God can flow through them. Your heart must be supernaturally transformed to carry the love of God.

Supernatural love cannot flow through a natural heart. Electrical power cannot be conducted through insulators. It is also unadvisable to pass electrical current through an appliance that has not got the capacity to handle it – it will blow up.

God Is Love

The love of God has no hatred in it. It is pure. God is light and in Him is no darkness at all. It is impossible to be unmixed in the natural sense. But the love of God is completely unmixed. God does not hate His creation. He loves the worst sinner though He hates his acts.

God has not got love – God is love. If you have something you can lose it, or give it up, but if you are something it cannot be taken from you. Human beings have the love of God so we sometimes lose it. God is love and He cannot lose Himself.

John, the Apostle of love gives us a glimpse of the love of God in his epistle.

> *Beloved, let us love one another: for love is of God; and every one that loveth is born of God, and knoweth God.*
> *He that loveth not knoweth not God; for God is love.*
>
> *1 John 4:7-8*

John said that love is of God. This means more than the fact that love comes from God. It actually means that God is the originator of love. There can be no love outside God. Anybody who loves, is born of God. The presence of love in our hearts is like the use of DNA tests for scientific verification of things. DNA tests can be used to prove fatherhood. In the same way love can be used to prove the fatherhood of God. Nobody can walk in true love without God. Anyone who loves is born of God and knows God. If we claim to know God because of our "righteousness" and spiritual gifts but we don't love people, we deceive ourselves – we don't know God.

God is love. Everything about God is love. Look at God from

any angle and He is love. You have ears but you are not ears. Looking at you from a certain position may not reveal your ears but your legs. God is love. From any angle God is love. His acts of forgiveness speak about His love. God's deliverances portray His love. Acts of healing, provision, miracles, salvation and favour all demonstrate the love of God. If we look at God from the angle of His chastisements and judgments, we still see nothing but love. Love pervades everything God is and does.

God loves the undeserving.
God's love is unconditional.
The love of God is unending.

The love of God seeks and pursues us. It does not wait for us to come to it. God would do anything to have you. God has not given up on you. Your life is precious in His sight. We need an assurance of God's love in our days more than ever before. We are surrounded by so many enemies, difficulties and dangers that thousands of believers are becoming disillusioned. New doctrines are springing up everyday, which make us more vulnerable to the enemy. These doctrines don't have God at the centre of your life. You are made to look helpless in the hands of the devil.

God loves you and He would do everything possible to save you.

> Since thou wast precious in my sight, thou hast been honourable, and I have loved thee: therefore will I give men for thee, and people for thy life.
> Isaiah 43:4

We are precious in God's sight. He loves us and this guarantees our deliverance.

On Thursday, 21st September, 2006 I was in my office when one of the young men who works in the general office dashed in and announced to me that he was sending one of our pastors to the hospital. I enquired why and he said that the pastor had just been involved in an accident on his motorbike on the streets just in front of our church. The driver of a car who happened to be one of our church members ran into him as he tried to negotiate a turn. The impact of the collision was so great that the pastor was thrown off his bike. The car trapped the motorbike between its front tyres and made its way towards the pastor who was rolling away to safety. The driver in her panic stepped on her accelerator instead of her brakes and headed towards the helpless pastor. He saw the vehicle coming towards him and he wondered what was going to happen. At the end of the episode he saw the car go off in a different direction with the motor bike still trapped underneath its front part.

The Lord delivered the pastor from death in a very dramatic way. Few people escape death in accidents like this. To avoid being crushed by an advancing vehicle by rolling away is a miracle. Maybe he was rolling faster than the car. When I visited him later on he said that there was a rumor in town that he vanished when the car hit him. I laughed and told him that as much as people could be exaggerating what happened, he might have actually vanished.

The pastor in question is the pastor in charge of our rural missions. He is a very good man. I believe that God loves him and the people he is dedicated to ministering to, so He delivered him from death. The love of God reaches out to us anywhere, anytime to deliver us from the schemes of the devil. Our generation which is operating in the midst of wickedness needs the assurance that God is with us.

In times of deliverance it is very easy to understand the love of God. It is however, very difficult to comprehend the love of God when negative things hit us in the face. The apostle Paul assures us that nothing can separate us from the love of God. He holds us so close to Himself that no attack of the enemy can snatch us from His care and protection. The challenges we face every now and then can make us doubt the love of God. I have been hit by things that almost shook my belief that God loves me. The storms of life can bombard the very foundations of our faith in God. The word of God is very clear about the fact that nothing can separate you from God's love.

> Nay, in all these things we are more than conquerors through him that loved us.
>
> For I am persuaded, that neither death, nor life, nor angels, nor principalities, nor powers, nor things present, nor things to come,
>
> Nor height, nor depth, nor any other creature, shall be able to separate us from the love of God, which is in Christ Jesus our Lord.
>
> Romans 8:37-39

Speaking from his personal experience and the things that confronted the believers of his time daily, Paul declared that we are more than conquerors through Him that loved us. Paul is persuaded that neither death, nor life, nor angels, nor principalities, nor powers, nor things present, nor things to come, nor height, nor depth, nor any other creature shall be able to separate us from the love of God.

The things listed above include both good things and bad things. It is obvious that good things like life are more likely to draw us closer to God than bad ones like death. What the great apostle is conveying to us is that the love of God is not dependent on circumstances. You cannot use your circumstances to determine whether God loves you or not. In times of bereavement, job loss, difficulties in ministry and marriage frustrations it is very easy to doubt the love of God.

To appreciate the love of God we must look at the big picture and not focus on the isolated incidents of our lives. If you consider the overall picture of what God is doing in your life, you can only conclude that God loves you and that He is a good God.

God loves us and He will never leave us nor forsake us.

God loves us and forgives our sins. He blots out our transgressions and our sins He remembers no more. Don't allow a weak conscience to bring up sins you have confessed and repented of to torment you. Jesus said to the woman caught in adultery that He did not condemn her. Refuse to allow the devil to convince you that you will continue to suffer setbacks in life because your ancestors or parents have sinned against God. The Jews asked Jesus whose sin made a man to be born blind. Jesus' answer was that no one sinned but the blindness was an occasion for God to be glorified. Don't allow the devil to use your past sins or the sins of your ancestors as an excuse to invade your blessed life.

The forgiveness of sins is one of the most important things about the love of God. The devil has always tried to undermine this aspect of God's love. The religions of the world are struggling with the issue of sin and its forgiveness. They do ablutions and torture their bodies with the hope that they can deal with their sins. It will be a tragedy for the Church to doubt God's ability to forgive and deal with sin. To doubt this is to give the devil the power to steal, kill and to destroy.

Understanding the love of God empowers us to live a high quality life in Christ. It also gives us the guide to living with other people. God is love and we cannot live a godly life without appreciating the love of God. If God is love it means that everything about God and godliness is love.

If you don't love people, you don't know God. Believers erroneously place emphasis on good works. They try to serve

God but they don't love their fellow humans. Preachers love the ministry but not the people. They are addicted to the motions of the ministry but are indifferent to the souls of the ministry. They love the crowd but not the individuals that make up the crowd.

Love is everything and this makes it imperative for us to stop everything we are doing that is not connected to love and pursue the ways of love.

CHAPTER 2

LOVE IS EVERYTHING

God is love and this alone should make us know that love is everything. God is everything to us. In Him we live, move and have our being. All things are made by Him and without Him is nothing made that was made. He is the beginning and the ending. God is light and in Him is no darkness at all. Jesus is the author and the finisher of our faith. There can be no life, world or advancement without God. He that cometh to God must believe that He is. God is. He is everything you would ever want Him to be.

God is the all-sufficient God. He is our shepherd. Jehovah is our healer and giver of peace. The LORD is our banner. Our sanctification comes from Him. He is the jealous God who protects us from evil. He is ever present with us – He will never leave us nor forsake us. These and many more are the magnificent things God is and does. God can do none of the above things and He can be none of the above to us without love. God's ability to perform and His willingness to bless us lies in His love. For instance, God had a Son who could die and save us, but He would not have given Him for us without love. God so loved the world that He gave His only begotten Son.

God's actions are wrapped up in His love. In the same way all our deeds and life are worthless in God's sight if they are not enveloped in love. Love should not just spice our deeds. That can easily lead to hypocrisy and pretence. Love must be the essence of our being. Love must be the spirit of our deeds. It should be the reason for which we do things and the force behind every godly deed and activity.

❖ The Qualities Of Love

1 Corinthians 13 shows clearly that love is everything. It demonstrates beyond any shadow of doubt that without love our deeds are worthless. In this great chapter of scripture love is also seen as the single spiritual virtue that embodies everything about the fruit of the spirit.

> *Though I speak with the tongues of men and of angels, and have not charity, I am become as sounding brass, or a tinkling cymbal.*
>
> *And though I have the gift of prophecy, and understand all mysteries, and all knowledge; and though I have all faith, so that I could remove mountains, and have not charity, I am nothing.*
>
> *And though I bestow all my goods to feed the poor, and though I give my body to be burned, and have not charity, it profiteth me nothing.*
>
> *Charity suffereth long, and is kind; charity envieth not; charity vaunteth not itself, is not puffed up,*
>
> *Doth not behave itself unseemly, seeketh not her own, is not easily provoked, thinketh no evil;*
>
> *Rejoiceth not in iniquity, but rejoiceth in the truth;*
>
> *Beareth all things, believeth all things, hopeth all things, endureth all things.*
>
> *Charity never faileth: but whether there be prophecies,*

they shall fail; whether there be tongues, they shall cease; whether there be knowledge, it shall vanish away.

For we know in part, and we prophesy in part.

But when that which is perfect is come, then that which is in part shall be done away.

When I was a child, I spake as a child, I understood as a child, I thought as a child: but when I became a man, I put away childish things.

For now we see through a glass, darkly; but then face to face: now I know in part; but then shall I know even as also I am known.

And now abideth faith, hope, charity, these three; but the greatest of these is charity.

1 Corinthians 13:1-13

The above scripture is one of the greatest scriptures on the subject of love. It is important to investigate the context in which Saint Paul introduces the subject of love. In 1 Corinthians 12 he deals with the gifts of the Holy Spirit and in 1 Corinthians 14 he speaks about the speaking in other tongues, which is a manifestation of the gifts of the Spirit. This means that 1 Corinthians 13, the love chapter is sandwiched between two chapters on the gifts of the Holy Spirit. It stands to reason that Paul is telling us that we should not practise spiritual gifts and neglect the practice of love – love is everything.

Paul exposes fifteen irrefutable characteristics of love. The kind of love Paul is dealing with is Agape. This is the God kind of love. It is the kind of love Jesus has for the Church. It is so divine that the devil and his people cannot have it. I will list these characteristics briefly:

Charity suffereth long – love is patient. Agape is not impatient. With Agape we are able to wait for our time. When our hearts are filled with Agape, we don't struggle with God and the spirit of covetousness does not consume our souls.

Charity is kind. Kindness is the force that moves a person to help his neighbour. It liberates us from religious pretence and empowers us to support one another. Kindness is a combination of mercy and positive action.

Charity envieth not. Agape thanks God when another person is blessed by God. True love is not jealous. Love eliminates the spirit of unhealthy competition from the Church.

Charity vaunteth not itself. Love is not boastful – it does not brag. Love does not dominate every conversation with words like "I am, I have, I know and it is me." Self promotion is not the attitude of love.

Charity is not puffed up. Love is not proud. Pride is the conceived exaggerated opinion of oneself. Many people don't see themselves in the perfect mirror of God's Word but in their self-made magnifying glasses.

Charity doth not behave itself unseemly. Love is not unmannerly. It is orderly. It respects time. Love is not disrespectful – it does not shout curses at people and swear at random.

Charity seeketh not her own. Love is not inward looking. Love reaches out to others – it bears the burdens of others.

Charity is not easily provoked. It does not easily flare up. Love does not react to situations and people on impulse. Love controls its emotions and this is reflected in the words it speaks and in its actions under pressure.

Charity thinketh no evil. Love does not keep record of evil done to it by others. It does not hold the wrong doing of others against them and judge them without cause later on. Judge not that ye be not judged.

Charity rejoiceth not in iniquity, but rejoiceth in the truth. Agape is not glad about wrong doing. Love has holy anger against evil. Love hates anything that exploits human beings. Love rejoices in the truth. The Apostle John was glad that his spiritual children walked in the truth.

Charity beareth all things. Love bears suffering silently. It does not blame others for its actions. Love does not defame others in order to justify itself. Love allows itself to be defrauded if that will bring peace and glorify God.

Charity believeth all things. Love believes in the honesty and integrity of others. Love propels us to build relationships based on trust. It is not suspicious of others.

Charity hopeth all things. Many faith people equate hope with unbelief. On the contrary hope is positive and not negative. Faith is the part of belief that keeps a man going today and now. But to stay alive until a promise comes to pass in the future one needs hope. Hope looks to the future and endures all things.

Charity endureth all things. Endurance is the ability to stay alive in the midst of trials and opposition.

Charity never faileth. The unending nature of love is the last and the greatest feature of love the Apostle mentions. Agape outlives all other virtues. When it is all over love will be the only thing that will be standing. Love is the ultimate expression of spirituality.

Having discussed the characteristics of love it is not difficult to figure out that love is everything. A close examination of 1 Corinthians 13 shows that love is the best and the greatest feature of God's nature which He has deposited in our hearts. It is greater than spiritual gifts. It is higher than other godly virtues.

❖ The Superiority Of Love

I. Love is the language of spiritual gifts.

Without love spiritual gifts are meaningless. They don't edify. Love is the factor that makes spiritual gifts speak with clarity. A spiritual gift is supposed to testify about the goodness of God and His power. Without love gifts don't express the limitless dimensions of the goodness of God. A gift without love is mere noise.

> *Though I speak with the tongues of men and of angels, and have not charity, I am become as sounding brass, or a tinkling cymbal.*
>
> *1 Corinthians 13:1*

It is very striking that Paul started by talking about the use of the tongue without love. He did this because many people love in word only but not in deed. To speak with the tongues of men and of angels refers to the gifts of utterance – speaking in other tongues, interpretation of tongues and prophecy. To do these without love is to be noisy without spiritual effect. Speaking with the tongues of men could also refer to making promises with our mouths, saying good things about people, speaking intelligently and powerfully or maybe speaking romantically to your spouse without love.

In the days of Paul there were many great orators who baffled the people with their oration and words. These people crept into the churches unawares and led the flock astray because many of them had itching ears. The apostle was warning them to place more emphasis on the love of a preacher than on his oratory. Don't allow anybody to take advantage of you with deceptive words.

29

Great promises of blessing and healing from a preacher should not make you allow him or her to take advantage of you.

There is too much noise in the church. This noise takes the form of meaningless words and the hypocritical uttering of things we don't understand. Broken promises, prophecies that never come to pass, misleading words and blatant lies have found their way into the Church. Our results are not congruent with our words. We say and do not. We speak and it does not come to pass. The world is becoming irritated by our noise. They don't see any manifestation that God is with us.

The Bible tells us not to love in word only. We are not to recite words in church without attaching any importance to them. It is very common to see anointed men and women of God, curse the same people they are called to bless. Out of bitter and wounded spirits the men and women of the pulpit release the venom of curses without love. When their curses destroy lives they don't worry about it. They rather boast that they are so powerful that their curses have come to pass. Jesus was not known for cursing people but rather for blessing them. Even on the cross He loved and blessed His enemies instead of cursing them.

Sounding brass (noisy trumpets) and tinkling cymbals (clanging cymbals) represent noise that is loud and yet has no content. It is high time we understood that oration without love is empty noise. Prophecies without love lead to exploitation of unsuspecting worshippers. Speaking in other tongues without love has denied the Church direction in many ways. Worshippers are confused because of the abuse of the gifts of the Spirit.

The sound of trumpets and clanging cymbals may be used for party calls and war alarms. If they make uncertain sounds nobody would gather for parties. If trumpets sound confused alarms during battles, an army would be thrown into disarray. The gifts of the

Holy Ghost are similarly employed to comfort God's people and prepare them for war. These gifts are operating below capacity in our time because of the lack of love. The exercising of these gifts is also plagued with confusion, competition and strife.

II. Love is the substance of faith.

If we exercise great gifts like faith, prophecy and knowledge without love we are nothing. Love is the substance of faith. Faith without love has no weight.

> *And though I have the gift of prophecy, and understand all mysteries, and all knowledge; and though I have all faith, so that I could remove mountains, and have not charity, I am nothing.*
>
> *1 Corinthians 13:2*

Faith moves mountains of opposition and removes obstacles from our way. Through gifts of prophecy, faith and knowledge we are able to overcome great obstacles and achieve unimaginable things for God. The achievement of great feats is a laudable thing to do but love should not be sacrificed in our bid to do great things.

Unfortunately, our generation has placed disproportionate emphasis on the achievement of great feats at the expense of love. We sacrifice people to attain our goals. We love the ministry and hate the people. The crowd gives us fulfillment but the individual person in the crowd is a nuisance to us.

We cannot stand the problems of an individual but the euphoria the crowd generates tickles our ego. If we remove mountains and have no love we are nothing.

There is no doubt that we have thousands of achievers in the house of God. Anointed men abound. Gigantic church buildings are going up everywhere. The ministry of deliverance is liberating millions of souls. Financial miracles are flooding the Church. We are indeed moving mountains. Christian authors are increasing. Exploits have flooded the Kingdom of God. These great things are happening at a time when the love of God is rare in the Church. Believers are living like unbelievers when it comes to demonstrating the love of God.

Love is everything. If we achieve everything and move all mountains and have no love we are nothing.

III. Love is the life of sacrifice.

Without love a sacrifice is a dead sacrifice and does not please God. Every sacrifice we offer to God must be a living sacrifice. Love is the only proof that our lives are in the sacrifices we offer to God and other people.

> And though I bestow all my goods to feed the poor, and though I give my body to be burned, and have not charity, it profiteth me nothing.
>
> 1 Corinthians 13:3

If we give all our goods to the poor and offer our bodies to be burned but have no love it profits us nothing. One may wonder how someone can do these two things and not have love. The reasons are simple. We can give our goods to the poor just in obedience to God or to receive the praise of men. We can also offer our bodies to be burned simply because others are doing so and we want to appear spiritual too. There are also people who do good just because they fear God's wrath and judgment if they don't do so. Finally, some people do good things because they think that those things will earn them tickets to heaven. Such motives are not pleasing to God. Sacrifice without love profits us nothing. Sacrifice without love does not produce lasting results.

Neither does it give one any eternal rewards.

God did not have respect for the offering of Cain because there was no love in his heart. The writer of Hebrews compared the blood of Abel with the sacrificial blood of Jesus. Abel's blood was spilt because he offered an acceptable sacrifice to God. Everything about Cain suggests that he did not walk in love. He was a murderer. He was bitter and arrogant. Because of the lack of love in him, his offering was rejected.

Ananias and Sapphira sold their land and brought the money to church. Unfortunately they kept back part of the price of the land. They did not walk in love because love gives all and not part. They were dishonest but there is no dishonesty in love. They gave to show off. They were men pleasers. They just wanted to look good in the sight of men and they attracted the instant wrath of God. Their offering profited them nothing.

David said that he would offer to God no sacrifice that cost him nothing. That is love. A costly sacrifice is not determined by the amount of money or the size of the sacrifice. It is determined by how dearly we regard what we are offering.

Love is everything. Serve the Lord with love. If we sacrifice our time, money, energy and even our lives but have no love it is a waste. This explains why there are so many unfruitful ministries though the ministers are laboring to death. Love provides the spiritual life of a sacrifice. It makes the sacrifice acceptable both to God and man. When people do things for us and there is no love in what they are doing we can tell.

IV. Love is the spirit of every godly character.

In 1 Corinthians 13: 4-8 the apostle Paul described the characteristics of love in detail. Amongst these great qualities are patience, kindness, humility, endurance, hope, faith and good manners. In terms of character love is everything – it is the spirit of every godly character. There can be no godly character without love.

From the above characteristics of love it is obvious that no one can have good character without love. Without love we cannot be patient. No one can be kind without love neither can we have good behavior towards others without love. When the Bible says that God is love what it means is that every attribute and nature of God is contained in His love. People who walk in love invariably display all the other good qualities of godly character.

Jonathan loved David and this affected the way he related to David. Jonathan did not seek his own interest – he was prepared to hand over his position to David. Jonathan did not behave himself unseemly towards David. He respected him and did everything possible to protect him from Saul's wrath.

Love is not proud or boastful. It is very common to find people (even in the pulpit) who are so boastful that they undermine everybody as they try to dominate them. Marriages are under threat as men and women refuse to submit to one another. Men abuse the headship God has given them and women rebel against what they call male chauvinism. In view of this expression of the lack of love the courtrooms are choked with believers who are trying to obtain judgments against their spouses. Orderliness and peace have deserted our homes. No one allows himself to be defrauded.

We are taught that we are the head and not the tail. I wonder how an animal can be only a head and have no tail. When the Bible says we are the head and not the tail it is referring to our relationship with the world. We are the head and the world is the tail. Nevertheless, in the house of God there must be a head and a tail. Everybody cannot be the head. The Bible makes it clear that the man is the head of the woman and Christ is the head of the man. This is however, not a license for the man to oppress the woman. He is rather supposed to love the woman as himself from that position. In a great house there are not only vessels of gold and silver but also of earth and wood. Again God has set in the Church firstly apostles, secondly prophets and thirdly teachers. We are positioned at different levels in the Church and the spirit of love enables us to submit to one another without pride.

V. Love is eternal – gifts will fail.

Charity never faileth: but whether there be prophecies, they shall fail; whether there be tongues, they shall cease; whether there be knowledge, it shall vanish away.

1 Corinthians 13:8

Love lasts forever, spiritual gifts don't. Spiritual gifts will disappear when Jesus comes again because all things will be perfect and we shall have no need of gifts. Love will survive the end of time because even then our relationship with God and other citizens of the eternal kingdom must continue eternally. Love is the factor that keeps every relationship working. Without love there can be no bond between God and us. We cannot live together as brethren without love. Our relationships must be founded on love and not on gifts.

In most churches members are not in the church because they love their pastor but because he has a spiritual gift they need. They are there because of what they can get. These worshippers lack the agape love of God – love which is not motivated by what it can get but by what it can give. If the pastor goes through a challenging time when the power and grace for ministry are not flowing as the members expect they leave the church and join another one. Many pastors are also guilty of pastoring congregations not because they love them but because of what they can get from them.

Many shepherds over God's people desert the congregation in search of greener pastures. They embellish their desertion by claiming that God relocated them. Teachers of the word of God must not minister only to people who can give them what they want. The gospel must be preached to the poor.

Churches and organizations that are established on love last longer than those that are founded on spiritual gifts and human charisma.

Everything is temporary but love is permanent. Don't pursue spiritual gifts at the expense of love. It is easier to lose your gifts than to lose your love. Don't labor for perishables at the expense of permanent things. We often say that the gifts and the callings of God are without repentance. This is true but it does not mean what people think. The gifts and the callings of God are always there but that does not mean that they are always working. Sometimes they don't work because they are not needed. That is why when Jesus appears and perfection comes we will not need the operation of gifts. Another reason why these gifts will not always flow is that sin, disobedience and hardness of heart block the flow. A lack of love is one of the main manifestations of a hard heart. Love never fails and in operating our spiritual gifts we must endeavor to walk in love – it is the only way to keep the gifts flowing.

VI. Love is whole – gifts are in part.

> *For we know in part, and we prophesy in part.*
> *But when that which is perfect is come, then that which is in part shall be done away.*
> *1 Corinthians 13:9-10*

The above verse makes it plain that prophecy is in part. It is not the whole thing. Prophecy is not everything. It covers some parts of our lives and some aspects of God's works and nature but not the entire scope of God's dealings with us. Not everything is given to us by God in prophecy. For instance, we cannot know God as He knows us through prophecy. Moses saw His back parts but not His whole figure. This means that prophecy is limited. Further limitation applies to prophecy because the human channel through whom the prophecy flows is not a perfect person. His own limitations affect the quality of the manifestation of the gift of the Holy Spirit. The Gifts of the Holy Spirit are in part – we know little thus the gift of prophesy is in part.

God is a God of perfection. When that which is perfect comes, that which is in part will disappear. Several interpretations have been applied to the term "that which is perfect". Some people believe that it refers to the completion of the New Testament. Others say that Paul meant the establishment of the new heavens and the new earth. A third group subscribes to the view that "the perfect" refers to the perfect state of the Church when Christ comes again. I believe that this third view is what Paul was referring to.

When the perfect dispensation comes the imperfect gifts will not be needed. In the perfect dispensation love will be the prevailing factor. The presence of perfect love will make every other thing unnecessary. Charity never faileth. Love is everything because even when that which is perfect comes love will remain.

VII. Love is the ultimate manifestation of maturity.

> *When I was a child, I spake as a child, I understood as a child, I thought as a child: but when I became a man, I put away childish things.*
>
> 1 Corinthians 13:11

One may not immediately see any reference to love in the above verse. If we however look at it in the context of other scriptures we would realize that childhood is the same as carnality. The Bible says that foolishness is bound up in the heart of a child (Proverbs 22:15). Paul called the Galatians foolish Galatians because in the search for more knowledge and revelation they exposed themselves to the works of the flesh (carnality) at the expense of the fruit of the Spirit (Galatians 3:1). A child is described as having foolishness. Similarly the Galatians are referred to as being foolish because of their carnality. By comparing scripture with scripture you see at once that childishness, foolishness and carnality are one and the same thing.

As children we speak as children – we place emphasis on the gift of speaking in other tongues. In this infantile state we also place great premium on understanding all mysteries – the gifts of revelation are our priority. Children are attracted to the sensational manifestation of gifts. In the childish state we think that spiritual gifts are everything – we think that as long as we can prophesy and move mountains we have arrived and we don't need anything more.

When we mature into adulthood we put away childish things. We place more emphasis on love and character. We combine the gifts of the Holy Spirit and the fruit of the Spirit perfectly. In the adult state love is manifested in exhibiting the gifts of the Spirit. When mature believers flow in the gifts of the Spirit the results are different from the results of immature people.

VIII. Love leads to a perfect revelation of God.

For now we see through a glass, darkly; but then face to face: now I know in part; but then shall I know even as also I am known.

1 Corinthians 13:12

The words "see through a glass" can be misunderstood to mean literally seeing through a glass. It however, means seeing as in a mirror. The reflection seems to the eye to be behind the mirror. In that case we see our image through the mirror. In the ancient times these mirrors were made of brass or other metals. The reflection of an object through a dim mirror always gives inadequate knowledge of an object compared to the knowledge obtained from a direct look at the object.

Dispensations are also alluded to in this verse. When the Church age is consummated and Jesus appears, we shall know God and the things of the Spirit as we are fully known by God. A simple example will help us to understand this. A relationship between a man and his wife is a progressive revelation. A man loves a woman and reveals himself to her and asks for her hand in marriage. In spite of the fact that she knows him, he does not expose his nakedness to her; neither does she expose herself to him. After their wedding vows they are sure of their love for each other. A covenant seals the relationship at their wedding. At this point they are now prepared to expose themselves to each other fully.

In the relationship between God and man, God is perfect and He knows all things. He does not have to wait for us to reveal ourselves to Him. He knows us directly but we know Him through faith, His Word and revelations. The amount of revelation we give people about ourselves depends on the extent of their love for us. In this church age we are not perfect in our love for God and one another. We therefore have limited knowledge of God and other believers. When this age is over and our love reaches perfection we shall see God as He is – He will reveal Himself fully to us because our love is perfect.

Your revelation of God can never rise above your love for God.

> *He that hath my commandments, and keepeth them, he it is that loveth me: and he that loveth me shall be loved*

*of my Father, and I will love him, and will manifest myself
to him.*
John 14:21

Jesus said two things were necessary for God to manifest Himself to
us. First, He manifests Himself to us because He loves us. Secondly,
He manifests Himself to us because we love Him. John 14:23
emphasizes the fact that God manifests Himself to us depending
on our love for Him. It actually says that the Father and the Son
will make their abode in us when we love God.

*Jesus answered and said unto him, If a man love me, he
will keep my words: and my Father will love him, and we
will come unto him, and make our abode with him.*
John 14:23

**We reveal ourselves to people when we know that they love
us. It is the same with God. The amount of His power and
blessing He allows us to carry depends on our love for God
and His people.**

Power and blessing can be abused if we don't have the love of
God. One reason why God reveals Himself to us based on our
love for Him is that knowledge puffs up. Love is not puffed up. It
is not proud. The abundance of revelation will not puff us up if
we walk in the love of God.

IX. Love is the greatest.
*And now abideth faith, hope, charity, these three; but the
greatest of these is charity.*
1 Corinthians 13:13

All gifts of the Spirit will keep dwindling in significance until they
disappear at the coming of the Lord Jesus. Three things will remain

when these gifts have ceased namely faith, hope and charity. Faith is trust in God. Without faith there is no creature and there is no God. God creates and man believes. In heaven we shall still have to trust God as the creator and sustainer of all things. The faith here is not the gift of faith for healing and deliverance but trust in God as our savior and maker.

Hope will also remain because we shall not possess all things at once. Heaven will be a place of progressive experience and revelation of the provisions of God. The greatest of the three things is love because both faith and hope are essential elements of love. We cannot have love without faith and hope. Love believes all things and hopes all things (1 Corinthians 13:7).

Faith and hope are intertwined with love because it is impossible to love without them. Recently I was talking to a couple that lost their young son. It was a very painful blow to them and they could not come to terms with it. They had many questions and their frustration was great. They had made covenants with God concerning the boy and when he died suddenly they were wondering what they had done wrong. I told this couple to keep trusting God because He is all knowing and all wise. I explained to them that coming from a prophetic ministry they were likely to think that they should know all things before they happen. They might also think that through their faith, they should be able to stop every misfortune from happening. It does not work like that always. We know in part and prophesy in part.

Because we know in part and prophesy in part, things take us by surprise sometimes. We go through things we can't understand and these things threaten our love for God and for one another. The only way we can keep loving God and other people even when things are not going well for us is to keep trusting God and hoping for the blessed day of resurrection He has promised.

The Church is plagued with perennial strugglers who want everything now and have no room for faith and hope. Love, faith and hope are the last three things that remain when all other things like our spiritual gifts and blessings are shaken. Amongst these three, love is the greatest.

The word "greatest" is the Greek word *meizon* and it means more, larger, eldest and greatest. Love is the greatest of all virtues because it encompasses every virtue of godliness. Love is like the whole thing in which every other thing is contained. Love is everything. From the above discourse life without love will leave us unfulfilled. Spiritual gifts are meaningless without love. The fruit of the spirit is hollow without love. Love is supreme. It is above all things.

It is imperative for us to walk in love and resist every temptation to live without the love of God in our hearts. Current trends reveal that Satan is working tirelessly to deny the Church the power to love. Hurts and offences are on the rise in families and churches. Believers are conjuring up good reasons to continue walking in bitterness and hatred. Because love is everything, the devil is attacking its existence in our hearts with various challenges. The things we go through daily try to rob us of the love of God. The early believers faced challenges that threatened the love of God in their hearts. The author of the book of Hebrews accordingly urges us to let brotherly love continue.

CHAPTER **3**

LET BROTHERLY LOVE CONTINUE

I often wonder why it is so difficult for us to love one another in the Church. Believers applaud the world for succeeding but hate one another's success. When the world performs great feats we admire them and say that it is the blessing of God. The arrival of similar blessings in other believers' lives however, provokes jealousy and resentment from us. Even at the pastoral level love is difficult to attain. It is very difficult to see a pastor rejoice at the breakthrough of another pastor. The spirit of competition is threatening the existence of love amongst us.

In the early days of the church the writer of the book of Hebrews urged the Hebrews to let brotherly love continue. The believers were practising the love of God but this love came under constant threat. The author of the book of Hebrews sought through intense exhortations to stir up the love in the hearts of God's people. He urged them to let brotherly love continue.

Let brotherly love continue.

Hebrews 13:1

The words "brotherly love" in the above verse is the Greek word *"Philadelphia"* which means **brotherly love, fraternal affection**

and brotherly kindness. This kind of love is phileo love. It is different from the *agape* love of God in that it is demonstrated to people who have a close relationship with us, whereas *agape* is shown towards those who may have nothing to do with us. *Philadelphia* is a product of *agape*. We cannot have *"Philadelphia"* when we don't have agape because even the brethren will offend us and tempt us to walk in hatred.

The word "continue" is the Greek word *"meno"* which means to stand, dwell, endure, tarry, continue and abide. It is interesting to note that the word "let" is also the same Greek word *"meno"*.

We could therefore render the above verse in a number of different ways.

Let brotherly love remain.

Let brotherly love endure.

Let brotherly love stand.

Let brotherly love abide.

Continue, brotherly love, continue.

Stand, brotherly love, stand.

The word *meno* is repeated for emphasis. Love was under severe threat and the author was admonishing the saints to continue to love. Love must survive our times. Love must endure the temptations of our day. Your love must stand the betrayals it is suffering daily.

We can always find good reasons not to walk in love. Over the years I have arrived at the conclusion that the most difficult thing to do in the Church is to let brotherly love continue. Several factors combine to make it difficult for us to love one another.

We must overcome these factors and walk in love because to love one another is a commandment. Jesus commanded His disciples to love one another.

> *A new commandment I give unto you, That ye love one another; as I have loved you, that ye also love one another.*
> *By this shall all men know that ye are my disciples, if ye have love one to another.*
> *John 13:34-35*

We are to love one another as Christ loves us. Our love for one another is supposed to measure up to the love Christ has for us and not less. It is through loving one another that people will know that we are the disciples of Christ. The hatred amongst us betrays God's nature.

We had a case in our church in which two of our members working in the same place quarrelled with each other so much so that they caught the attention of the authorities of their work place. Everybody knew that they were members of our church. The enemies of Christ and of the church took advantage of the situation. They abused us and the name of Christ was brought into disrepute. These ladies constituted a stumbling block in the way of their colleagues who could have been saved. All efforts by our church and the work place of these sisters to unite them yielded no positive results. We finally suspended them from active service in the church whilst we continued to make efforts to bring them together. As I write this book they are now on talking terms and have a meaningful relationship with each other.

We must endeavor to let brotherly love continue. In Hebrews 13:1- 9 the Bible shows us some of the obstacles we must overcome to let brotherly love continue. The verses after the first one mention certain situations that require a demonstration of the love of God.

Let brotherly love continue.

Be not forgetful to entertain strangers: for thereby some have entertained angels unawares.

Remember them that are in bonds, as bound with them; and them which suffer adversity, as being yourselves also in the body.

Marriage is honourable in all, and the bed undefiled: but whoremongers and adulterers God will judge.

Let your conversation be without covetousness; and be content with such things as ye have: for he hath said, I will never leave thee, nor forsake thee.

So that we may boldly say, The Lord is my helper, and I will not fear what man shall do unto me.

Remember them which have the rule over you, who have spoken unto you the word of God: whose faith follow, considering the end of their conversation.

Jesus Christ the same yesterday, and today, and for ever.

Be not carried about with divers and strange doctrines. For it is a good thing that the heart be established with grace; not with meats, which have not profited them that have been occupied therein.

Hebrews 13:1-9

The challenges that faced the early Church reveal the need for love. These challenges presented good excuses for people not to walk in love. For instance, it was very easy to dwell on the misconduct of a previous visitor and refuse to receive a new visitor into one's home.

Let us consider some of the challenges of the time and see how they threatened the love of the brethren.

Overcoming Love Killers

There are several factors that militate against love. The early Church like today's Church was confronted with challenging situations which made it difficult to walk in love. For brotherly love to continue believers have to overcome the love killers amongst us.

❖ Be not forgetful to entertain strangers.

The Bible enjoins us not to forget to entertain strangers (Hebrews 13:2). This admonition is in reference to travelers who were sent on assignment. Some people might have abused the privilege of being hosted by others. It is not unusual to receive charlatans and pretenders into your home. After such experiences we don't want to entertain strangers anymore.

Apart from homes, churches receive all kinds of people who come in the name of the Lord. Some receive visitors who come in and seduce women sexually. They even lure married men and women away from their spouses. Acts of deceit, stealing, fraud and dishonesty are rampant in homes and churches. The havoc caused by some visitors is so much that many well meaning believers and churches are not ready to receive visitors into their homes.

The writer of Hebrews however, admonished the Church that in spite of such despicable acts by some unscrupulous elements, brotherly love had to continue. He cited a biblical precedent of some people receiving angels unawares. I believe that this exhortation was in reference to the Jewish story of how Abraham received three visitors, at least two of whom turned out to be angels (Genesis 18:1-14). Lot also received angels into his house (Genesis 19:1-2).

The main visitors the author of the book of Hebrews was advising the believers to receive were missionaries who carried the gospel from one place to the other. The inns were very expensive in those times and a lot of criminal and immoral acts were practised there.

It was therefore wise for the saints to be entertained in homes. This privilege was likely to be abused by visitors, forcing brethren to refuse to receive visitors into their homes.

Such a move was likely to affect the spreading of the gospel. The author of Hebrews was reminding the believers that they should not discard the practice of entertaining visitors because there was the possibility of missing angelic visitations in their bid to avoid unscrupulous strangers. Besides some of the messengers of God were carriers of genuine anointings and we need them in our lives.

The Shunammite woman compelled Elisha into her home and she received a miracle son. She was also forewarned of impending famine by the prophet and she migrated to save her life. Upon her return to Israel after the famine, her inheritance was restored to her. The widow of Zarephath similarly received Elijah the prophet and she experienced the miracle of the multiplication of oil and flour. Her son was also raised from the dead by the man of God when he died.

We are admonished to receive and bless strangers.

Wash the feet of the saints.

Give strangers food to eat.

Bring them in and pray for them.

I remember many years ago I went into town in Bolgatanga and found a mentally ill guy. He was dirty and there were sores all over his body. I was a student in the University at that time and I was living with a Christian brother in his apartment. After preaching to this mentally ill guy one day, I led him to Christ and with the permission of my host I moved him into the apartment. We prayed for him and cleaned him up. This guy lived with us for some time and joined a Bible believing church. He later became a preacher and worker of the kingdom of God. This is a typical example of entertaining strangers. We must move out of our comfort zone and embrace people of other races and denominations.

We shall be called upon to entertain people we don't know too well. To do this we must have the discernment to receive people by the spirit. Nabal refused to receive David because he did not have the spiritual capacity to recognize the next king of Israel who was trapped in the wilderness.

> *And when David's young men came, they spake to Nabal according to all those words in the name of David, and ceased.*
>
> *And Nabal answered David's servants, and said, Who is David? and who is the son of Jesse? there be many servants now a days that break away every man from his master.*
>
> *Shall I then take my bread, and my water, and my flesh that I have killed for my shearers, and give it unto men, whom I know not whence they be?*
>
> *1 Samuel 25:9-11*

Nabal undermined the grace of God on David's life and the Lord smote him to death. Nabal's pride denied him the wisdom and discernment to take advantage of the opportunity to meet David who was to be the king of Israel.

> *But it came to pass in the morning, when the wine was gone out of Nabal, and his wife had told him these things, that his heart died within him, and he became as a stone.*
>
> *And it came to pass about ten days after, that the LORD smote Nabal, that he died.*
>
> *1 Samuel 25:37-38*

Nabal missed his due time. This kind of due time is called the "kairos moment". The word Kairos is the Greek word for

due time, season or opportunity. The "kairos moment" is an appointed time in the purpose of God. It is a season in which God acts. We must take advantage of every opportunity to embrace an angel.

Love takes us beyond the familiar and makes us believe good things about people who are complete strangers to us.

A word of caution is however important at this point. There are scriptural reasons not to accept some kinds of people in our homes or fellowship. An example of such is people who carry false doctrines. The Bible admonishes us not to receive them or wish them God speed.

> *If there come any unto you, and bring not this doctrine, receive him not into your house, neither bid him God speed:*
> *For he that biddeth him God speed is partaker of his evil deeds.*
> *2 John 1:10-11*

We are to walk in love but there are spiritual ways to know the kind of people to receive. As much as possible every visitor we receive must have a credible point of reference. The stranger must also bear the fruit of godly character and have a sound doctrine. Another thing to look out for is whether you have peace in your heart or not. Don't hoard dubious characters in your home in the name of love. If we don't know the strangers at all and there is no way of checking on them we should put them up in hotels and monitor the exposure we give them before the flock of God. It is the responsibility of a shepherd to protect the flock from ravenous wolves. No matter the situation we find ourselves in, however, we should avoid treating strangers with contempt. Even in refusing to offer assistance to a stranger for very good reasons we should do so politely and lovingly.

❖ Remember them that are in bonds.

In Hebrews 13:3 the author admonished the Hebrews to remember the believers who were in bonds. These believers were thrown into prison for their faith. Persecution coupled with the imprisonment of the saints could easily threaten the bond of love amongst the brethren. This compelled the writer to urge them to let brotherly love continue.

In many parts of the world life-threatening forms of persecution still persist – people are killed, imprisoned, poisoned, thrown to wild beasts and ostracized from society. In other parts of the world more subtle forms of persecution take place. It is gross ignorance to think that there are believers anywhere on earth who are not going through any form of persecution. Even in the free and democratic society of the USA believers are going through various forms of persecution. In some places the saints are thrown out of their worship places, development plans of cities are designed to favour other religions, the press is used to destroy the testimony of churches and pastors and laws are formulated to deny the Church expression in issues that matter to us.

In situations where persecution and imprisonments persist many things happen to break down the unity amongst the brethren. A few of such things are the following:

Betrayals are likely to be on the increase. It is common to see believers betray one another for what they can get. Persecution provides good business for the perverted ones amongst us. Judas Iscariot took advantage of the Jews' hatred for Jesus and sold Him for thirty pieces of silver.

Believers are unwilling to visit those that are in bonds for the fear of being associated with them.

We neglect visiting the saints in prison and pretend to be busy preaching the gospel in our own comfort zones. In the days of Paul some people actually intensified their preaching when Paul was in prison just to add pain to his bonds.

Those in prison lack basic amenities. We can easily shun their company because we don't want to share our worldly goods with them.

It is also worth noting that when people are in prison they deteriorate in many ways. It is very tempting to shun them because they don't look or smell good.

The butler forgot about Joseph when he came out of prison. The author of Hebrews told his readers to remember those who are in bonds. They are to empathize with them and live as if they are bound with them. As a body we should not isolate ourselves from the sufferings of others. In general the modern day Church does not face the crude form of persecution the early Church faced. We however, face our own situations that expose the lack of brotherly love in the Church. We do not visit the sick. When brethren who were once rich lose their wealth, even the pastor stops checking on them. Brethren face misfortunes only to be deserted by their loved ones in the house of God.

We should not join the world to persecute our own. When the world rises up against some of our brethren we must have the wisdom to protect our own. Let brotherly love continue. Look for the lost amongst us. Weep with them that weep. Share the pain of them that are in pain. It is very agonizing to be in pain and have no one share it with you.

To be in bonds is to be in pain and to be restricted. There are many spiritual, physical and mental restrictions we are subjected to. Some churches and even marriages are prisons. Injustice and torture take many forms. We must find ways of bringing comfort to those that need it. It is wrong to indulge in all our pleasures when others are languishing in pain.

Besides believers who are in bonds we have to reach out to prisoners in general. Even the unbelieving in prison need our love. There are countless testimonies of people who were saved while in prison and came out to make impact in the body of Christ. In the Bible Onesimus was converted by Paul when they met in prison.

Imprisonment should not separate us. Persecution must not stop us from being responsible for one another. Let us do church together even in prison.

❖ **Marriage is honorable in all.**
Marriage is one of the institutions in which the love of God is most vividly demonstrated and tested. The marriage union is an ideal description of the relationship between Christ and the Church. Most people who are not married feel a sense of loneliness and unfulfillment especially if they don't have the grace to be celibate. A Christless life is similarly, a hopeless life. A bad marriage introduces great pain into people's lives. It is therefore common to see Satan employ every available strategy to deny believers the opportunity to marry. He also works tirelessly to destroy existing marriages.

In the days of the early church some people taught the superior purity of the state of celibacy. This is where some denominations derive their inspiration to deny ministers of God the right to marry. The author of the book of Hebrews states very clearly that marriage is honorable and the bed is undefiled. Marriage is to be held in honor amongst all believers whether they are ministers or ordinary brethren in the Church.

Marriage is an avenue to share one's life with another person. It is an arena in which the love of God is manifested towards a spouse and children. In spite of the nobility of marriage some people thought that if they left their marriage partners and stayed single they would serve God better.

In I Corinthians 7 Paul admonished the saints not to leave their spouses for the sake of the ministry.

> *Now concerning the things whereof ye wrote unto me: It is good for a man not to touch a woman.*
> *Nevertheless, to avoid fornication, let every man have his own wife, and let every woman have her own husband.*
>
> *1 Corinthians 7:1-2*

The saints wrote to Paul concerning marriage. They wanted to know whether it was proper to marry in the present circumstances of the Church. Paul reasoned that it was good for a man not to touch a woman, nevertheless to avoid fornication it was better for every man to have his own wife.

The connection between marriage and "philadelphia" (brotherly love) is obvious, because a person's spouse is one of the closest people to him. Marriage is one of the aspects of our lives in which we experience the greatest love. It is also the place in which the deepest hurts and wounds are inflicted on people. Adultery, divorce, abuse and denial of conjugal rights are some of the areas in which we torture one another in marriage.

It is very easy to opt out of marriage unions just to obtain our freedom. We may wish to do so because our partners are unbelievers or because we think that we can serve God better when we are single. Paul told the Corinthians that they ought not to divorce their spouses in order to serve God. If they separated from their partners they were not to remarry.

And unto the married I command, yet not I, but the Lord, Let not the wife depart from her husband:

But and if she depart, let her remain unmarried, or be reconciled to her husband: and let not the husband put away his wife.

But to the rest speak I, not the Lord: If any brother hath a wife that believeth not, and she be pleased to dwell with him, let him not put her away.

And the woman which hath an husband that believeth not, and if he be pleased to dwell with her, let her not leave him.

1 Corinthians 7:10-13

Paul was single himself but he esteemed marriage very highly. We cannot fully explain the relationship between God and man without looking at the relationship between husband and wife. Paul told the Ephesians that a man ought to love his wife as Christ loved the Church and gave Himself for it.

Husbands, love your wives, even as Christ also loved the church, and gave himself for it;

That he might sanctify and cleanse it with the washing of water by the word,

That he might present it to himself a glorious church, not having spot, or wrinkle, or any such thing; but that it should be holy and without blemish.

So ought men to love their wives as their own bodies. He that loveth his wife loveth himself.

For no man ever yet hated his own flesh; but nourisheth and cherisheth it, even as the Lord the church:

Ephesians 5:25-29

Men are to love their wives as their own bodies. The above scriptural reference says that he who loves his wife loves himself. This must drive us to take another look at marriage. The love revolution must begin from our marriages and homes. Women must discover the love in submission. When women submit to their husbands they are not debasing themselves. Rather they are demonstrating the love of Christ because He made Himself of no reputation and laid down His life for us all.

In another place Paul told Timothy that in the selection of widows for ministry in the church, he should ensure that they were looking after their families well and providing for them.

> *But if any provide not for his own, and specially for those of his own house, he hath denied the faith, and is worse than an infidel.*
>
> 1 Timothy 5:8

Paul placed great premium on marriage and family. Our love for our families is very crucial. Don't refuse to provide food for your family with the claim that you are using your money to build the kingdom of God. We must not spend all our time in prayer meetings and church services to the neglect of our families. If we are unable to take care of our families the way we should, we have denied the faith and we are worse than infidels. It is unfortunate to see families break down and we must do our best to hold our homes together. Children should love their parents and be in subjection to them. Parents should not provoke their children to wrath.

We cannot claim to love God when we hate our own flesh. Paul said in Ephesians 5:29 that no man can hate his own flesh. To hate your spouse and claim to love God is deception. A man stopped going to church because his wife hated him and yet she stood in front of the church every Sunday pretending to serve God. The man could not stand the contradiction so he fell out of fellowship.

If we love our spouses as ourselves some things will show:

We don't cheat on them.

We don't deny them conjugal rights.

We provide for them.

We refrain from abusing them.

We endeavor to stay united to them – we don't do things that lead to separation.

We don't embarrass them privately or in public.

We are ready to die for them.

Marriage is honorable and it is good for believers to marry. Failure or refusal to marry when it is obvious that one has to do so can lead to adultery and fornication. The author of the book of Hebrews sought to convince the believers that marriage was honorable and not ignoble. He was trying to debunk the false impression that was spreading, which suggested that celibacy was always more honorable than married life.

❖ Avoid covetousness.

If "philadelphia" is to continue amongst us we must eschew covetousness. Love is a giver and covetousness is a grabber. It is impossible to combine these two in one's life. Until we learn to be content with what we have, we cannot love the brethren. The rivalries and jealousies amongst believers are on an alarming increase. At the church level, church rivalry is scary. We snatch members from other churches without apology. We rush to acquire wealth and properties just because others have them. We want the fame others are enjoying. We want wives and husbands like theirs. The progress of other people stirs up a demon of envy in us.

Within our churches the story is no different. Associate pastors want everything their Senior Pastors have. They want the pulpit because they think that they are better preachers and teachers than the Senior Pastors. Members are covetous and withhold their tithes and offerings from the Church. Senior Pastors are greedy of filthy lucre. The abuse of power and exploitation of members is the order of the day. The report of the Church amongst unbelievers is not good.

We must realize that we cannot enjoy certain privileges when it is not our time. Elisha did not enter the whirlwind (with the chariot and horses of fire) that took Elijah into heaven. The chariot and horses of fire parted the two men asunder.

> And it came to pass, as they still went on, and talked, that, behold, there appeared a chariot of fire, and horses of fire, and parted them both asunder; and Elijah went up by a whirlwind into heaven.
>
> *2 Kings 2:11*

Elisha could not have joined the whirlwind and chariot because Elijah had finished his assignment and was ready to go to heaven. Elisha on the other hand was not ready for heaven. He had the wisdom to ask for a double portion of the spirit of Elijah and not the chariot from heaven. The chariot represented heavenly dignity and honor. Elijah was honored by God because he had completed his task. Elisha was yet to begin. If Elisha had joined the whirlwind (with the chariot) he would have been partaking in honor he did not deserve. Again the whirlwind would have taken him to heaven before he even began his assignment. Elisha would have gone to heaven instead of towards the river Jordan to begin his exploits with the mantle that fell to him.

It is important we realize that we cannot join certain chariots. These chariots separate us from others who have gone ahead of us. There are blessings you will not receive now because they are rewards God gives to those who have excelled in ministry.

We must be humble enough to appreciate this fact.

Love is not covetous. In the early times of the Church, just like today, people were covetous when they saw others being blessed. They just wanted things but life is more than the acquisition of material things.

It is not what you get that is crucial but what you can use. There is no point in grabbing things only to be unable to use them.

A simple example can illustrate the folly of covetousness.

One evening during our teaching assembly in Bolgatanga, I gave a simple illustration of the folly of covetousness. I took a carrier bag from home and put a lady's African long skirt with the matching top in it. The owner of this attire is my niece who lives with my family. She is a little lady. On the night in question I was teaching on the subject of covetousness. At a certain point during my teaching I called a lady from the congregation who is also smallish in structure and one of our protocol men who carries the physique of a giant. I told them that I was going to throw the carrier bag into the air and if either of them grabbed it, the person had to use the contents of the bag. I knew that the big protocol guy would catch it. When I threw the bag into the air he snatched it from the reach of the lady as I suspected. I then told him to open the bag and use the contents. When he opened it he discovered that he could not use the contents, because they were lady's attire. Another problem was that they were too small to fit him even if he were a lady.

Covetousness may make us receive things we cannot use after all. Gehazi received the material things of Naaman the leper but I believe that he could not use them well. Elisha cursed him with leprosy and he could not have enjoyed the clothes he received from Naaman.

Judas Iscariot betrayed Jesus for thirty pieces of silver but he could not use the silver. He committed suicide and the money went to waste. He could not purchase the land he intended to use the money for because it was accursed money.

The answer to covetousness is to be content with what we have. Godliness with contentment is great gain. The key to living a life of contentment is the knowledge that Jesus will never leave us nor forsake us. Brotherly love (philadelphia) is only possible when there is no covetousness. The sons of Jacob could not have "philadelphia" because of jealousy and covetousness. In the love revolution we must remove covetousness from the Church.

After cautioning the Hebrews about the dangers of covetousness, the author of the book of Hebrews zeroed in on another love killer. This love killer is fear. In the same text of Hebrews 13:1-9 the author mentions other things we must watch in our pursuit of love. Let us be patient enough to explore some other issues this great author raised regarding the subject of brotherly love.

CHAPTER 4

OTHER BROTHERLY LOVE KILLERS

For love to flow in our hearts certain spiritual factors are crucial. The fear of man must leave our hearts and our revelation of God must be applied to our way of life. Our perception of people also has a great effect on the way we live. You cannot love people if you are either suspicious of them or afraid of them. Understanding the unchanging nature of God explains the constancy of His love for us. **God's love is immeasurable because He is immutable.** Another thing which is of interest to us in the text under consideration is the issue of doctrine. I am convinced that the incursion of strange doctrines in the Body of Christ is largely responsible for the collapse of brotherly love in the Church.

❖ There is no fear in love.

Quoting from Psalm 118:6 the author of Hebrews said in Hebrews 13:6 that: "So that we may boldly say, The Lord is my helper, and I will not fear what man shall do unto me."

Fear is a love killer. You cannot love someone you fear. Many people carry with them hurts of the past that make them live in perpetual fear. Married people fear their spouses. Bosses don't trust their subordinates and subordinates feel terrorized by their bosses. The fear of evil and anxiety about the future combine to make the love of many for God cold.

Fear paralyses love and hinders us from releasing our gifts and talents for the blessing of others.

Commitment to the vision of ministries is seriously affected by some common fears which plague many organizations these days. The fear of being cheated and exploited kills commitment. The fear that someone may use us and dump us prevents us from sacrificing ourselves for a cause.

The parable of the unfaithful servant shows the effect of fear on performance. He went and hid the talent his master gave him because he was afraid of him. His actions earned him sharp condemnation from his boss. The fear of the servant was based on some preconceived ideas he had about his boss – he believed that his boss was exploitative. His fear was also predicated on the fact that he did not appreciate what he had. This fearful servant could not love because instead of appreciating what he had he was jealous about what the other servants had.

> *Then he which had received the one talent came and said, Lord, I knew thee that thou art an hard man, reaping where thou hast not sown, and gathering where thou hast not strawed:*
>
> *And I was afraid, and went and hid thy talent in the earth: lo, there thou hast that is thine.*
>
> *His lord answered and said unto him, Thou wicked and slothful servant, thou knewest that I reap where I sowed not, and gather where I have not strawed:*
>
> Matthew 25:24-26

The above servant denied his boss the harvest because of fear. His colleagues who received five talents and two talents multiplied them, but the wicked and slothful servant buried his talent. He was afraid and this made his master call him wicked. A wicked person is one who does not walk in love. To withhold your gifts from others is lack of love because love gives. It is common to see intelligent people refuse to make contributions to discussions during meetings because they are afraid that they would be rebuked if they made mistakes.

Several years ago a friend who was a pastor approached me with a problem he was having with the General Overseer of his ministry. He was of the opinion that his Overseer was a controlling person who loves to own everything and manipulate everybody. He told me that his church was not growing as it ought to. He made it clear that he could have done something about it but his boss is a hard man. He thought that if any serious growth occurred in the church his boss would remove him and bring someone else to take over the church. This friend of mine later on took the church through embarrassing crisis and left to start his own ministry. He did not walk in love because he was afraid of his General Overseer. This negative attitude can also be found in homes and businesses.

There is no fear in love. The Bible says that perfect love casts out fear. He that has fear is not made perfect in love. The fear of man blocks the flow of love in our hearts.

> *There is no fear in love; but perfect love casteth out fear: because fear hath torment. He that feareth is not made perfect in love.*
>
> *1 John 4:18*

For brotherly love to continue we must do away with fear. Hebrews 13 also raised the issue of spiritual leadership. It is interesting to see how good leadership and teaching are related to our flow in the love of God.

❖ **Remember them that have rule over you.**

In our pursuit of brotherly love we have to examine the lives of the saints who have gone ahead of us. The writer of the book of Hebrews admonished the Hebrews to remember the faith and manner of life of the leaders and teachers who had taught them the word of God.

> *Remember them which have the rule over you, who have spoken unto you the word of God: whose faith follow, considering the end of their conversation.*
> *Hebrews 13:7*

The mention of "them which have rule over you" in the above verse has to be explained. The category of people the author of Hebrews is referring to is leaders (rulers, guides) whom God had set over the Hebrews. Leaders play crucial roles in the wellbeing of the people God places under them. **Two of these roles are governing them and teaching them.** The function of leadership under consideration, with reference to Hebrews is not the oversight or governing role of leadership but the teaching function. This is clearer when we consider this verse in other translations of the Bible.

> **Remember your former leaders—it was they who brought you God's Message.** *Bear in mind how they ended their lives, and imitate their faith.*
> *Hebrews 13:7 (WEYMOUTH NEW TESTAMENT)*

> **Remember your leaders who have taught you the Word of God.** *Think of all the good that has come from their lives, and try to trust the Lord as they do.*
> *Hebrews 13:7 (THE LIVING BIBLE)*

> **Remember your leaders who first taught you the word**

of God. Think of all the good that has come from their lives, and trust the Lord as they do.
Hebrews 13:7 (NEW LIVING TRANSLATION)

The author of Hebrews pointed to the faith and end of conversation of the leaders who first taught the Hebrews the word of God. The mention of their faith and end of conversation seems to suggest that some of them might have died probably through martyrdom. The Hebrews were to consider the lives of men and women who like Stephen and James the brother of John, loved the Lord so much that they gave up their lives.

Such leaders did not serve God for personal gain. One of the most practical ways to walk in love is to keep our focus on people who walk in pure love. Probably, this admonition was crucial because a breed of leaders were beginning to show up either from outside or amongst themselves, who had a selfish agenda for the ministry.

New breeds of leaders often introduce new trends into a movement that are very different from the original plan. Whereas the founders of movements are usually selfless, future ones may seek to take advantage of existing opportunities to satisfy their lusts.

I have encountered many ministries where the spirit of covetousness in new leaders completely betrayed the selfless spirit of the founding leaders. It is imperative for us to keep our focus on the founding fathers of Christianity because of the uncountable cases of bad examples around us. Today's politician is different from yesterday's leader. The modern day preacher is different from the ancient holy man of God.

Most nations were founded by selfless leaders only to fall into the hands of greedy politicians in the future who have no love for human life. Businesses have experienced unfortunate times when succeeding CEOs lacked the love and commitment of the business founders.

"The end of the conversation" of the leaders who first taught the Hebrews the word of God refers to the end result of the lives of the early teachers. They lived and died for others – they did not live for themselves. Their motive for serving the saints was spiritual satisfaction and not personal material gain. God never forsook them even in death. The love of God motivated everything these leaders did for God and His people. The Hebrews were to let brotherly love continue by emulating the leaders who had gone ahead of them.

Hebrews 13 introduces the subject of the immutability of Jesus in the admonition for brotherly love to continue. It says that Jesus Christ is the same yesterday, today and forever. I often hear preachers and teachers use this verse to talk about the power of God for healing and deliverance. This is both scriptural and needful. They however, fail to connect the love factor. The main reason for mentioning the immutability of Jesus is the love of God and not the power of God. The Church of our time is so hungry for the power and blessing of God that we fail to consider the operation of the love of God amongst us.

❖ **Jesus Christ the same yesterday, and to day, and for ever.**
The author of Hebrews takes a very interesting turn when he introduces a line of scripture about the unchanging nature of Jesus Christ. All along he had been talking about what the brethren had to do to walk in love. Suddenly, he switched to the perfect example of love – Jesus Christ the Son of the living God. He said that Jesus Christ is the same yesterday, today and forever.

> *Jesus Christ the same yesterday, and to day, and for ever.*
> *Hebrews 13:8*

Jesus Christ does not change and that guarantees the constant flow of His love. The subject of change is crucial to our discussion on the love of God. God loves always because He does not change. Charity never fails because the God of love does not change.

Malachi said emphatically that God does not change.

> *For I am the LORD, I change not; therefore ye sons of Jacob are not consumed.*
> *Malachi 3:6*

The prophet indicated strongly that God does not change and that is why the sons of Jacob were not consumed. God had made a covenant with Israel and He was not going to change His mind in spite of Israel's waywardness.

The world is ever changing and so are the people in it. People are so unpredictable in our day that it is not advisable to depend on their promises and commitments. Worshippers change into sinners overnight and righteous people metamorphose into idolaters right under the crystal chandeliers of churches. God's love does not fail under the severest test. The vacillating nature of man does not disturb the orientation of God's heart. God loves His people even when they are wayward. He may chastise them for their sins but He never leaves them nor forsakes them.

"Philadelphia" cannot continue if we respond to the disappointments people spill our way every time. The only way love can stay in a marriage is if couples decide never to change. Brotherly love cannot continue in churches if we respond to the wrongs others commit against us. The resolve not to change is key to our ability to stay in love.

The language of love is very revolutionary:

"I will love you no matter what you do to me."

"It is impossible to hate you."

"I simply cannot hate you."

"I can forgive everything and anything."

The key to the constancy of God's love for us is that He is the same yesterday, today and forever. This must be the case with us. We cannot be the same yesterday, today and forever; only God is. Nevertheless, we must make the effort to walk as He walked. We must follow in God's steps.

David the man after God's heart is noted for his love for people. He even loved his rebellious son Absalom after he rebelled against him. When Absalom died in battle one would have expected David to rejoice but he rather lamented the death of his son.

> *And the king was much moved, and went up to the chamber over the gate, and wept: and as he went, thus he said, O my son Absalom, my son, my son Absalom! Would God I had died for thee, O Absalom, my son, my son!*
> *2 Samuel 18:33*

One might think that David lamented over the death of Absalom simply because he was his son. We however, know that when Saul and Jonathan died he lamented greatly for them also. David did not change even when the opportunity to become the next king of Israel showed up, after the death of Saul. He could have rejoiced about the opportunity to become king but he chose to love. Too many people change when opportunities show up.

> *The beauty of Israel is slain upon thy high places: how are the mighty fallen!*
> *Tell it not in Gath, publish it not in the streets of Askelon; lest the daughters of the Philistines rejoice, lest*

the daughters of the uncircumcised triumph.

> *Ye mountains of Gilboa, let there be no dew, neither let there be rain, upon you, nor fields of offerings: for there the shield of the mighty is vilely cast away, the shield of Saul, as though he had not been anointed with oil.*
>
> *2 Samuel 1:19-21*

David saw the death of Saul as a loss to Israel and himself. He did not rejoice at the fall of his enemy. If God wanted David to be king He could do it without embarrassing the kingly anointing of Israel on the mountains of Gilboa.

The lives of others must take precedence over our personal opportunities. Don't allow the opportunities to be rich or successful change your loving nature. Don't sacrifice other people on the altars of your success. You should not be denatured in your bid to be successful.

In his zest to sustain brotherly love amongst the brethren, the author of Hebrews introduced another crucial subject that had to do with the new doctrines some teachers were carrying.

❖ **Doctrines of hatred and discrimination.**

The connection between sound doctrine and love is not difficult to deduce. Religions of hatred are founded on strange doctrines. Some doctrines of devils command their adherents to kill in the name of God. In history even groups that profess Christianity have murdered and committed genocides in the name of God. Suicide bombers and terrorists have multiplied in the name of Islam.

It is very easy to assume that these doctrines of hate exist only in extremist sects and cults. An objective and sincere examination of the modern day Church, however, reveals some startling situations. We discovered earlier on that amongst the early believers a false doctrine of the superiority of celibacy over married life tried to entrench itself. This doctrine brought with it the tendency for people to abuse their spouses and even separate from them. Zealots thought that by living single lives they would be able to serve God better.

The inspired scribe of the book of Hebrews warned against strange doctrines that militated against the operation of brotherly love amongst the saints.

> *Be not carried about with divers and strange doctrines. For it is a good thing that the heart be established with grace; not with meats, which have not profited them that have been occupied therein.*
> *Hebrews 13:9*

People can sometimes be so preoccupied with their doctrines that they hate others who don't share their views. To impose your beliefs on others is a lack of love. The Jewish believers felt a sense of superiority over gentile believers and sought to compel them to embrace the Mosaic Law. Love is founded on grace and not strict religious laws.

The doctrine of "taste not and touch not" was going around.

> *Wherefore if ye be dead with Christ from the rudiments of the world, why, as though living in the world, are ye subject to ordinances,*
> *(Touch not; taste not; handle not; Which all are to perish with the using;) after the commandments and doctrines of men?*
> *Colossians 2:20-22*

Some portions of the Mosaic laws were smuggled into the faith and imposed on gentiles by apostles and believers with unrenewed minds. A certain breed of teachers walked away from the spirit of grace and peddled other doctrines that emphasized salvation by works. The main purpose of the "doctrine of meats" (clean and unclean) is to make the Jew superior to the gentile. Brotherly love cannot continue if we follow these kinds of doctrines.

> There is neither Jew nor Greek, there is neither bond nor free, there is neither male nor female: for ye are all one in Christ Jesus.
>
> Galatians 3:28

The other side of this doctrine is anti-Semitism, which is also a dangerous doctrine. Hatred of the Jewish race is very strong in certain parts of the world. They are killed and segregated with some of their enemies even vowing that the state of Israel should be annihilated.

Doctrines which discriminate against people based on skin color, ethnicity, political affiliation and sex destroy the flow of love in the Body of Christ.

Racial and ethnic discrimination hinder love. The doctrine of Christ makes both the Jew and Greek one. Believers have refused to marry partners God was leading them to marry on ethnic grounds. In some parts of the world we have black churches and white churches. This unfortunate trend has denied the Body of Christ its full complement of power and strength. Discrimination against women is one other area of grave concern. Women are denied their place in the things of God. Violence against women is on the ascendancy. Women are used as objects to satisfy the lusts of men. If brotherly love will continue in the house of God, we must treat everybody equally.

Let brotherly love continue. It should be obvious by now that it is not easy to walk in agape love. Love is a God thing. It does not flow naturally out of a human heart. The love of God is shed abroad in our hearts by the Holy Ghost. There is a renewal that is taking place. It is a renewal of the hearts of God's people which is immersing them in the love of God. This renewal is not a general trend but some people are beginning to catch it. The pretentious forms of love are being overthrown. Love unfeigned must take over from hypocritical love. Our love should be of the highest quality; it must be love unfeigned. The love revolution is coming into your heart.

CHAPTER 5

UNFEIGNED LOVE

The love we demonstrate towards one another must be **unfeigned love**. As a matter of fact to talk about unfeigned love is a form of tautology because love cannot be insincere or pretentious. True agape love is not pretentious. There can be no insincerity in love. The apostles Paul and Peter mentioned unfeigned love in their teachings because some people might have attempted practising **"pretentious love."** There is widespread practice of pretentious love in today's Church.

> *By pureness, by knowledge, by longsuffering, by kindness,*
> *by the Holy Ghost, by love unfeigned,*
> *2 Corinthians 6:6*

The Greek word for love in the above verse is *agape* – the highest form of love. Unfeigned is the Greek word *anypokritos* which means without dissimulation, without hypocrisy. Paul was reminding the Corinthians about the spirit with which he and his compatriots in ministry ministered unto them. Amongst other things he said that they ministered unto them with purity, the knowledge of God, patience, kindness, the power of the Holy Ghost and love unfeigned.

Ministers and God's People

Ministers of God must minister to God's people without hypocrisy. The Bible is replete with examples of people who ministered to God's people with pretentious love. The sons of Eli ministered to temple worshippers with hypocrisy. They did not love God and this reflected in their attitude towards the worshippers. They took advantage of the people who came to the temple to seek God and enriched themselves. They made themselves fat by abusing their position in the temple.

> *Now the sons of Eli were sons of Belial; they knew not the LORD.*
>
> *And the priests' custom with the people was, that, when any man offered sacrifice, the priest's servant came, while the flesh was in seething, with a fleshhook of three teeth in his hand;*
>
> *And he struck it into the pan, or kettle, or caldron, or pot; all that the fleshhook brought up the priest took for himself. So they did in Shiloh unto all the Israelites that came thither.*
>
> *Also before they burnt the fat, the priest's servant came, and said to the man that sacrificed, Give flesh to roast for the priest; for he will not have sodden flesh of thee, but raw.*
>
> *And if any man said unto him, Let them not fail to burn the fat presently, and then take as much as thy soul desireth; then he would answer him, Nay; but thou shalt give it me now: and if not, I will take it by force.*
>
> 1 Samuel 2:12-16

The sons of Eli did not know God. They robbed the people and even took sacrifices that belonged to God. They took what they wanted before God's portion was offered to Him. They sent their servants with fleshhooks of three teeth. The servants of the pretentious priests under training struck the fleshhooks into the pan and whatever it brought up they took for the priests. **The Bible says that they took the offerings by force.** These sons of Eli wore priestly garments but their hearts were choked with the leaven of covetousness.

Some preachers today have their own fleshhooks of three teeth with which they manipulate people. These three teeth are pretentious words of man's wisdom, false signs and wonders and deceptive appearances.

Scriptures are twisted to keep people in bondage so that they will keep coming to church. False signs and wonders are unleashed to impress followers. These signs and wonders may not be wrong but they are so emphasized that we lose our concentration on matters of purity and godly living. Worldly methods are used to give ministry a deceptive gloss that attracts carnal worshippers.

Love is the greatest proof that the nature of God is flowing through us. Sadly though believers have abandoned the pursuit of love, and they are obsessed with material things. The love of God is supposed to advertise us to the world. When this fails believers employ the money factor, in an effort to draw towards them the attention of the world. Huge sums of money are pumped into publicity and the acquisition of physical and material things. Through these things preachers try to convince people that God is with us.

It is important to note that there is nothing wrong with motivating people with the scriptures to give money to the work of God. Signs and wonders are also a blessing to the Body of Christ. The physical and material developments of the Church are laudable. The problem is when these things are pursued not for the good of the people but to inflate the ego of ministers.

Shepherds are supposed to love the flock but the sons of Eli did the exact opposite. It is common these days for preachers to collect prayer requests from people with money in envelopes. This practice has been abused by many preachers who simply take out the money and do not bother to pray for the people. The preachers don't even see the prayer points. Such preachers pretend to love the people but their attitudes betray their words. We have many modern-day sons of Eli around.

Jesus spoke about the leaven of the Pharisees. This leaven is the hypocrisy of the "princes of the temple" – the Pharisees. Jesus took a swipe at the Pharisees by saying that they invade widows' houses and for pretence they make long prayers. To the unsuspecting widows these representatives of God came to relieve them of their pain, but they had a different agenda. Such apostles of greed come in with the aim of devouring the material things belonging to the widows and sometimes they lure these poor victims of death into sexual bondage.

> *Woe unto you, scribes and Pharisees, hypocrites! for ye devour widows' houses, and for a pretence make long prayer: therefore ye shall receive the greater damnation.*
> *Matthew 23:14*

The Pharisees prayed long but the prayers were pretentious. Their prayers earned them condemnation instead of heavenly reward. They prayed long and hard but there was no love in the prayer. One would think that a widow should attract the love of people instantly but the Pharisees were more interested in themselves than the widows.

Samuel provides one of the most sterling cases of integrity in leadership. His love for those he ministered to was sincere.

> *Behold, here I am: witness against me before the LORD,*

and before his anointed: whose ox have I taken? or whose ass have I taken? or whom have I defrauded? whom have I oppressed? or of whose hand have I received any bribe to blind mine eyes therewith? and I will restore it you.

And they said, Thou hast not defrauded us, nor oppressed us, neither hast thou taken ought of any man's hand.

1 Samuel 12:3-4

Samuel challenged Israel to bear witness against him if he had taken any man's ox, donkey or money by fraud. The people responded that he had defrauded no one. I wonder how many leaders can put themselves through this test. As God ignites the love revolution a new breed of leaders will arise with the Samuel kind of leadership.

Besides the challenge of ministers not loving the flock, the lack of love for pastors from the congregation is alarming. Congregations demonstrate a lack of love for their pastors under a number of circumstances:

- **When the pastor and his family are blessed by God with material things and favour, some members get grieved and even leave the church.**

Jealousy is a love killer and we must avoid it. It is proper for churches to seek the well being of their pastors. Recently a pastor took me to a beautiful house his church had assisted him to buy – this is a manifestation of love. Some pastors are not as blessed as this pastor. Several years ago I visited a church where some members left the church because the pastor had received a gift of a car from a benevolent person. When I asked some of the people who left, they told me that they did not think that the pastor deserved a car. The interesting thing about this thing was that the disgruntled members themselves had cars.

- **When the pastor is not ministering to their satisfaction, the lack of love from members is made manifest.**

The pastor's members compare him with other preachers in town, and leave for other churches where they think they can get what they want. Loyalty is a lost virtue amongst believers. They go to church to get something and if they fail to obtain that thing at a time they expect, they leave the church.

- **Another occasion for the demonstration of a lack of love comes when the pastor falls into sin.**

It is not a good thing for a pastor or minister to fall. Nevertheless when they fall they need our love and not condemnation. The Church has majored in killing our giants who fall into sin. We don't give them any chance for restoration – we simply deny them resurrection. A short while ago, I was involved with a congregation who refused to forgive their pastor for falling into sin. The church suspended him and arranged for him to be counseled. He was taken off the pulpit for not less than nine months. The church refused to give the pastor another chance even after he had humbly gone through the discipline they put him through. They threw him out in a very bad manner against my advice. I urged them to find an honorable way to relieve their pastor of his position even if they did not want him and they ignored my advice and booted him out. They thought that the pastor was staining their image as a church.

- **When a pastor falls sick some members desert him.**

Such church members don't want to share the pain of the pastor with him. They want a church where everything is fine. There are countless cases where ministers were taken ill, sometimes over a protracted period. Some congregations are very supportive in times like this. In other cases most of the members just pack and leave the church. I know of two cases where congregations stood by their pastors during prolonged illness. Unfeigned love remains resolute when times are bad.

- **Public attack of the pastor's integrity and ministry can make some members flee.**

Jesus said that if the shepherd is smitten the sheep would scatter. The devil knows this and so he uses the public to attack ministers of the gospel. The public capitalizes on minor mistakes leaders make to destroy their work. Lies are fabricated to mar his image and kill the confidence of his flock in him. Traps are set up to take pastors unawares and sometimes they fall into them. Congregations must love their pastors strongly enough to stand with them when their testimonies are attacked by mischievous people. In the love revolution we shall refuse to crucify our generals when they are under attack.

- **Some churches kick out their pastors when they no longer need them.**

It is a sad thing when pastors lose their cutting edge. Members push them out and go hunting for new heroes. This happens when pastors are aging and when they go on retirement. I am not suggesting that pastors should occupy pulpits even if churches are dying as a result of that. What we have to do in such cases is to help the pastor to come out with a succession plan for his replacement. He can also vary the way ministry is carried out in the church so that he receives enough assistance to keep the fire burning. I witnessed a case where a retirement process was not properly done and it nearly killed the pastor. The church literally took everything from the pastor and left him in misery. I must add at this point that pastors who find themselves in situations like these, have to cooperate with the church in humility for solutions to be obtained for the problems.

- **Correction and discipline from a pastor can make the congregation rebel against him.**

Some churches hate rebuke and correction. They don't like to be told the truth. If the pastor speaks the truth even in love, they hate him. Many churches have been left to live in sin, without the pastor having the moral courage to correct members. The shepherds of the flock feared that if they rebuked the congregation, they would be persecuted. In the love revolution churches must learn to receive correction with grace.

A case of unfeigned love – David and Jonathan

In the preceding discourse we saw a biblical example of a lack of unfeigned love in the sons of Eli. It is worthwhile to look briefly at a few cases of the operation of unfeigned love. Unfeigned love is pure – it is unmixed and without pretence. This kind of love is fervent – it continues without ceasing, it is earnest.

> *Seeing ye have purified your souls in obeying the truth through the Spirit unto unfeigned love of the brethren, see that ye love one another with a pure heart fervently:*
> *1 Peter 1:22*

Unfeigned love is not common but it is possible. Jonathan and David provide us with a classic case of unfeigned love. This case shows us the features of unfeigned love and stirs up our spirits to desire it. Jonathan loved David as his own soul.

> *And it came to pass, when he had made an end of speaking unto Saul, that the soul of Jonathan was knit with the soul of David, and Jonathan loved him as his own soul.*
> *And Saul took him that day, and would let him go no more home to his father's house.*

Then Jonathan and David made a covenant, because he loved him as his own soul.

And Jonathan stripped himself of the robe that was upon him, and gave it to David, and his garments, even to his sword, and to his bow, and to his girdle.

1 Samuel 18:1-4

The features of the unfeigned love of Jonathan for David are as follows:

His soul was knit with David's soul.

He loved David as his own soul.

Jonathan and David made a covenant.

Jonathan took his robe and gave it to David.

He gave David his garments.

Jonathan gave his sword to his new friend David.

Jonathan gave David his bow.

He also gave David his girdle.

The items Jonathan gave to David were symbolic of the depth of his love for David. Jonathan and David entered a covenant of brotherhood and this friendship demonstrated love in a most powerful way. Jonathan's soul was knit to that of David – they were of one spirit.

- **Motivation for the relationship**

The motive for this covenant relationship was love. Unfeigned love has no ulterior motives. When you love someone with unfeigned love you don't love the person for what you can get out of the relationship. You love for love and not for things. Anthony Robbins, an American Author, speaker and peak performance expert captured this idea of love in a powerful way. He said that:

"Some of the biggest challenges in relationships come from the fact that most people enter a relationship in order to get something: they're trying to find someone who's going to make them feel good. In reality, the only way a relationship will last is if you see your relationship as a place that you go to give, and not a place that you go to take."

A British psychiatrist, Anthony Storr also observed that:

"It is only when we no longer compulsively need someone that we can have a real relationship with them."

• **The Ceremony**

The ceremony of ratification involved Jonathan decorating David with certain essential items of his dressing. He parted with his garments and other things that were symbolic of his personhood to seal the relationship. Jonathan was ready to part with everything to make David what he had to be. There was no holding back in the relationship. Love unfeigned must go all the way to prefer the other person above yourself. In the love revolution we will discover that most of what we call love is not love after all – there is too much selfishness amongst us.

Let us look at the symbolism of the items Jonathan gave to David in 1 Samuel 18:1-4:

The Robe and the Garments – The robe was Jonathan's princely robe and the garments were his personal inner garments. They bore the monogram (design of letters interwoven) of his name. By giving these items to David, Jonathan literally gave his external glory and internal identity to David. What he was saying by this act was "I share all that I have and am with you; you can have everything including my throne."

The Sword – This was the warrior's badge of highest honor. Jonathan was telling David that they were not in competition. Unfeigned love does not compete. It rather seeks the success of the other person. It is strange to see so much competition amongst even married couples and family members. Unfeigned love is a rare thing and we should stop pretending that we love one another and ask God for a love revolution.

The Bow and the Girdle – it is said that these were the most sacred and secret treasures of personal apparel in an oriental wardrobe. To give these to David meant that Jonathan had no insecurity – he stripped himself of everything.

Through this display of unfeigned love Jonathan empowered David. Unfeigned love leads to the empowerment of the saints whereas the pretentious form of love kills our gifts and denies us expression.

David was empowered in many ways through the love of Jonathan:

1. Change of position.

The covenant between Jonathan and David ended the latter's stay in the wilderness with sheep. He was instantly ushered into the king's palace and given a position of responsibility and privilege. David met Jonathan and that changed his life completely. In times of difficulty, the person you meet can change your destiny overnight.

It was Saul who earlier on took David to the Palace but his position was consolidated by the unfeigned love of Jonathan. Saul took David into the palace but Jonathan ensured his stay in the palace. Saul admired David but Jonathan loved him.

Unfeigned love promotes others above ourselves but pretentious love seeks to elevate ourselves above everyone else. When people talk about themselves too much, they don't have unfeigned love. To find unfeigned love in a friend is one of the most powerful blessings you can ever receive.

Ben Stein, an American professor said:
"Personal relationships are the fertile soil from which all advancement, all success, all achievement in real life grows."

Anthony Robbins says it this way:
"The quality of your life is the quality of your relationships."

Strategic relationships determine everything about our lives. We must find people who love us enough to enter covenant relationships with us. In these relationships we should seek to be the givers and not the receivers because givers are superior to receivers.

David was not only promoted. He also received the impartation of honor. Respect and dignity came to the shepherd boy as soon as the anointed garments of the king's son fell into his hands.

2. Impartation of honor.
Honor was imparted to David at once when Jonathan put his garments on him.

Honor is different from a position. One can have a position without honor. Position is a placement but honor is how one is treated in that place.

Jonathan protected David and guided him to behave wisely in the king's palace. David had no previous exposure to palace life so Jonathan must have walked him through the basic routine of princely conduct. Through the act of giving David his garments he identified with David. Your change would come swiftly by an honorable person imparting his honor to you. When honor is bestowed on you, respect you did not earn comes to you.

Positions, abilities and gifts are useless without honor. Andrew Carnegie the American industrialist and philanthropist puts it this way; **"No amount of ability is of the slightest avail without honor."**

Besides giving David a position and bestowing honor on him, Jonathan opened doors of opportunity for him. Position and honor are not enough to let you make impact – doors or opportunities must be created.

3. Opening of great doors.

The covenant relationship opened doors of opportunity for David. He began to carry out assignments on behalf of King Saul. Jonathan must have allowed this to happen. I believe that he even initiated some of them.

> *And Jonathan stripped himself of the robe that was upon him, and gave it to David, and his garments, even to his sword, and to his bow, and to his girdle.*
> *And David went out whithersoever Saul sent him, and behaved himself wisely: and Saul set him over the men of war, and he was accepted in the sight of all the people, and also in the sight of Saul's servants.*
> *1 Samuel 18:4-5*

Napoleon Bonaparte, the French General and Emperor, perfectly understood the connection between ability and opportunity. He said; **"Ability is of little account without opportunity."**

Jonathan's love for David gave him the opportunity to eventually become the king of Israel. Unfeigned love discovers and develops great people. Without unfeigned love our relationships with one another will be fruitless. It is important for us to realize that we must not enter serious relationships with people unless we are sure of the operation of unfeigned love in the relationship.

The marks of unfeigned love

• **Unfeigned love does not faint.**

It is constant no matter what the other person does against you. Unfeigned love is not fragile. Most of us can remember some individuals we love to the point where no matter what they do we still love them. What a world of love we would have if we could extend this grace to everyone and not just a few people. Personally there are people in my life whom I love so much that the wrongs they do against me don't count. One cannot do anything about this kind of love. You simply love the person and nothing can break it.

• **Unfeigned love is not fake.**

Pretentious love makes false promises and gives false hopes. It is shrouded in secrecy. Don't develop a serious relationship with a person who seems to have too many things he or she is hiding from you. Some people have a fake smile and suspicious look. A smile on the face of some people can immediately tell you that their love is not real. The smile is forced. It appears twisted because it does not synchronize with the actual intentions of the heart.

Jealousy is one of the things that produces fake love. Have you ever presented good news to a friend and observed a weird look on his face? Fake lovers use people to achieve their aims and dump them. People have married fake people only to shatter their lives. Beware of fake love.

- **It is not forced.**

Love is not forced to do anything. It is purely voluntary. Don't rush into marriage with somebody who is almost forced to decide to marry you. In ministry or business refrain from entering partnership with anybody who thinks he is doing you a favour by aligning himself with you. Unfeigned love is not fastidious. It does not use fleshly criteria to select who it relates to. Jonathan was a prince but he chose to have a covenant relationship with David. Jesus humbled Himself and came down to our level.

- **Unfeigned love does not find fault.**

It ignores many things. It does not condemn. It is difficult to have a relationship with people who always find fault with you. Sometimes when there is none they create them and put them on you. Pretentious love blames you for everything that goes wrong. Jesus loved the woman caught in adultery and refused to condemn her. This self-righteous generation does not know anything about the love of God. We are busy stoning people who are caught in adultery without paying heed to the weightier matters of the law.

Love is everything and the kind of love that pleases God and makes impact is unfeigned love. Paul talked about the uselessness of sacrifice without love. It is therefore important for our labour to be the labour of love. Anything short of that is unacceptable to God.

CHAPTER 6

THE LABOUR OF LOVE

*B*efore we proceed to investigate the subject of the labour of love, it is important to understand what it is not. The labour of love is not merely determined by the amount of suffering or pain we experience whilst offering our services. We discovered earlier on that if we offer all our goods to feed the poor, and give our bodies to be burned but we don't have charity, it profits us nothing. The labour of love refers to labour which is not motivated by emotional love and lust. The labour of love is never directed at pleasing man, neither is it aimed at building human kingdoms. The labour of love is about Jesus and not man.

> *Remembering without ceasing your work of faith, and labour of love, and patience of hope in our Lord Jesus Christ, in the sight of God and our Father;*
> *1 Thessalonians 1:3*

The labour of love refers to labour motivated by love for the Lord and the brethren. Such labour is characterised by a massive display of faith and is anchored in the patience of hope in our Lord Jesus. The labour of love is done in the sight of God and not man. It is not aimed at pleasing man.

The Bible shows several types of labour of love. We shall look at some of them so that each one of us can be motivated to serve God in our own way. You will soon realize that the labour of love means more than what you think.

Types of labour of love

- **Loving the Lord**

This is the first labour of love. The Bible commands us to love the Lord with all our hearts, souls, strength and mind. We are also to love our neighbours as ourselves. Looking at the amount of effort we must put into loving the Lord, it is logical to conclude that to love is an act of labour. To do something with all your strength implies that energy is expended in the process. One of the most difficult things to do is to truly love God and people.

> *And he answering said, Thou shalt love the Lord thy God with all thy heart, and with all thy soul, and with all thy strength, and with all thy mind; and thy neighbour as thyself.*
>
> *Luke 10:27*

The psalmist likens his pursuit of God to the hart panting for the water brooks. To reach the water, the hart must search for it, sometimes by running from one place to another. It must overcome obstacles on its way. The distractions posed by other attractions must not divert the course of the hart; it must reach the water.

> *As the hart panteth after the water brooks, so panteth my soul after thee, O God.*
> *My soul thirsteth for God, for the living God: when shall I come and appear before God?*
>
> *Psalm 42:1-2*

To pant after God involves a few things. It involves **longing** for God, **leaning** towards God, **learning** the ways of God and **laying** down one's life for God.

- **Feeding God's flock**

Jesus told Peter that if he loved Him, he should feed His lambs.

> *So when they had dined, Jesus saith to Simon Peter, Simon, son of Jonas, lovest thou me more than these? He saith unto him, Yea, Lord; thou knowest that I love thee. He saith unto him, Feed my lambs.*
> *John 21:15*

This manifestation of the labour of love is consistent with the Old Testament promise, that God would give His people pastors after His own heart, who would feed them with knowledge and understanding.

> *And I will give you pastors according to mine heart, which shall feed you with knowledge and understanding.*
> *Jeremiah 3:15*

Feeding the flock of God involves several things which make it a difficult task. The pastor must hear from God in order to teach the Word of God. He should not just spill sense knowledge before God's people. The diligent pastor must tap into the mind of God and obtain revelation knowledge for the people. Another thing that makes feeding the flock difficult is that one must live what one preaches and teaches. This requires the price of discipline in one's personal life. The shepherd should love God and the flock enough to live right. Whenever a leader errs he places a stumbling block in the way of people who love him.

I also consider feeding the flock to be a labour of love because of the amount of study and research the pastor must make to provide in-depth and balanced teaching for the flock. The teaching of God's word can be very frustrating. Like most other kinds of the labour of love the recipients of the Word we preach may not even appreciate it. They might be unwilling to learn and remain stiff-necked.

In feeding the flock the shepherd must labour in the Word and in doctrine.

> *Let the elders that rule well be counted worthy of double honour, especially they who labour in the word and doctrine.*
>
> *For the scripture saith, Thou shalt not muzzle the ox that treadeth out the corn. And, The labourer is worthy of his reward.*
>
> *1 Timothy 5:17-18*

The Word of God requires us to give double honour to the elders that labour in the Word and in doctrine. Double honour consists of respect as well as material blessings we give to the men of God. The workman is worthy of his reward.

The calling to dispense the Word of God is the highest calling on earth, because it deals with the very souls of men and their eternity. The workman must rightly divide the Word and be uncompromising in his convictions.

> *Study to shew thyself approved unto God, a workman that needeth not to be ashamed, rightly dividing the word of truth.*
>
> *2 Timothy 2:15*

The labourer (toiler) of the Word must be diligent to show himself a person who rightly divides the word of truth. To divide the word of truth means to make a straight cut or dissect the word of truth. We must not be tempted to teach just our favorite themes in the Word of God and neglect essential aspects of it which we don't like. An unequal balance is an abomination unto God. To teach balanced word and rightly instruct God's people takes a lot of effort.

- **Intercessory prayer**

Intercessory prayer involves engaging heaven, the earth and hell in dialogue with the aim of establishing the kingdom of God. On Saturday 18th November, 2006 I was ministering in Hamburg, Germany and I received a word of prophecy in which the Lord said "I will release the armies of heaven and crush the horns of the city." By the armies of heaven God was talking about intercessors engaged by heaven for warfare on earth. Intercession is a labour of love. It is the demonstration of God's love to deliver His creation from Satan's control. We know about the negotiation skills of the officials of nations at war. What they do in the physical is what we do in the spirit. We speak until heaven gets its way on earth. We appeal to the counsels of heaven until the will of God is done on earth as it is in heaven. Individuals, families and nations have to be brought into the presence of God for discussion and this is exactly what intercessory prayer does. This kind of prayer is more intense than praying for our personal needs.

Intercessory prayer is a labour of love because the one we are praying for may not even know that we are praying for him – there is no eye service in intercession. It is also the labour of love because we don't aim at benefiting from the intercession directly.

Anna, the prophetess provides us with a classic case of an intercessor. Anna is mentioned in the Bible just after the inspired penman had captured the intriguing and amazing testimony of Simeon in

Luke 2:25-35. Simeon was a just and pious man who lived with the hope of seeing the redeemer before his death. Several ancient scholars believe that he was the son of Hillel, the great Jewish doctor and philosopher. God revealed to Simeon that he would not see death before the Messiah comes. When Jesus was taken to the temple, the Holy Ghost led Simeon there to bless God for His amazing gift to the world. The mention of Anna after Simeon is a strong indication that her devotion to God was one of a high standard.

> *And there was one Anna, a prophetess, the daughter of Phanuel, of the tribe of Aser: she was of a great age, and had lived with an husband seven years from her virginity;*
>
> *And she was a widow of about fourscore and four years, which departed not from the temple, but served God with fastings and prayers night and day.*
> *Luke 2:36-37*

Anna, the eighty four year old widow was deep in the things of God. She abounded in revelations and she might have spoken the word of God into people's lives, which explains why she was called a prophetess. This pious woman enjoyed married life for just seven years, having been a virgin before marriage. Upon the death of her husband, she devoted her life to fasting and prayer. In this divine service she might have fasted twice a week like the Pharisees. She also attended all public services in the temple – she did not depart from the temple.

To be dedicated to God at this level at eighty-four is a labour of love. Anna turned away from the attractions of the world and made herself a temple addict. Her labour of love was selfless. Her intercessory life was sacrificial – she did not demand anything in return like the sons of Eli did.

Some prayer warriors have been reported to charge people money and receive other material things from them in order to fast and pray for them. Ignorant church folks openly declare that they cannot fast and therefore hire others to do so for them. Prayer warriors who are engaged in this manner are not exhibiting the labour of love.

The apostle Paul mentioned Epaphras, saying that he labored fervently in prayers for the Colossians.

> *Epaphras, who is one of you, a servant of Christ, saluteth you, always labouring fervently for you in prayers, that ye may stand perfect and complete in all the will of God.*
> *Colossians 4:12*

The Greek word for "labouring fervently" is *agonidzomai*. The word connotes the idea of struggling (to compete for a price) or fighting. Intercessory prayer is fighting – it is a struggle to entrench the will of God on earth. The Weymouth translation of the Bible says that Epaphras was always wrestling in prayers on behalf of the church. Paul told the Colossians that Epaphras was always striving and agonizing for them in prayers.

Apart from intercessory prayer one other kind of prayer which can be regarded as a labour of love is the prayer of binding and loosing. The fact that some demons don't leave except by fasting and prayer should convince us that prayer is work. We must love people enough to labour in prayer until they are delivered from oppression.

> *Howbeit this kind goeth not out but by prayer and fasting.*
> *Matthew 17:21*

There are certain strong holds in people's lives that will not give way until someone is ready to pay the price in fasting and prayer.

- **Do good to your enemies**

All giving is not the labour of love. Most of the time when people give they expect something in return either from God or the person they give to. This kind of giving is not a labour of love.

> *But love ye your enemies, and do good, and lend, hoping for nothing again; and your reward shall be great, and ye shall be the children of the Highest: for he is kind unto the unthankful and to the evil.*
>
> *Luke 6:35*

It is normal to love our friends and relations. In the love revolution however, we are to love our enemies. Jesus said that we should lend money and things to people even if we don't hope that they would pay back. The blessing of this attitude is that our reward will be great and we shall portray that we are children of the Highest. God is kind to the unthankful and to evil people. When we do good to only those who show appreciation, our reward is on earth and God is under no obligation to bless us Himself.

When we don't do God's kind of good (doing good to the unthankful and to the evil), we receive blessings only at the human level. We cannot do man's kind of good and receive God's reward.

Help your enemies. Bless those who curse you. Forgive those who sin against you even if they refuse to repent. Do not repay evil for evil. It is common these days for even believers to avoid their own family members with the claim that they are evil. We are to overcome evil with good.

- **The ministry of giving**

The act of giving is one of the areas in which the labour of love is demonstrated. Paul admonished the Corinthian believers to abound in the grace of giving. He said that it was not enough to abound in everything and neglect the grace of giving.

> *Therefore, as ye abound in every thing, in faith, and utterance, and knowledge, and in all diligence, and in your love to us, see that ye abound in this grace also.*
>
> *2 Corinthians 8:7*

To give something to someone means that we are giving to that person what we have acquired through the use of our time, energy and brains. The use of our time, energy and brains implies that we have spent our lives to acquire the things we have. The value of the things we have is directly related to the amount and quality of our lives we put into acquiring them. When we give the things we have to people, we are actually giving them part of our lives.

When it comes to giving we must give until we give our very lives to others. We are to love one another as Christ loved us and gave himself as an offering and a sacrifice for us. There is a difference between giving oneself as an offering and as a sacrifice. An offering is a bloodless oblation – it is a gift presented to God which does not necessarily involve blood. A sacrifice on the other hand involves slaying, killing or slaughtering, that which we give to God. Christ did not only offer Himself; He actually sacrificed Himself – He laid down His life.

> *And walk in love, as Christ also hath loved us, and hath given himself for us an offering and a sacrifice to God for a sweetsmelling savour.*
>
> *Ephesians 5:2*

One of the most powerful gifts in the Church is the gift of giving. Everybody can give but there are some people whose giving is a gift from God – they give beyond themselves. Such people seize every opportunity to give and to do good unto others. We have some people in our church with this grace, who never cease to amaze me with their generosity. Such brethren have been a great source of encouragement to me as I seek to serve God in the northern part of Ghana. Generally the people in the region don't have much to give to the ministry but the faithfulness of a good number of them encourages me to go on. Giving to one another and serving one another is what Christianity is all about. We have to stop hiding behind Bible verses, which have no relevance to practical living and start facing the realities of life.

God demonstrated His love for us by giving us His only begotten Son.

> For God so loved the world, that he gave his only begotten Son, that whosoever believeth in him should not perish, but have everlasting life.
>
> *John 3:16*

There is no love without giving. This kind of giving is not selfish. It does not give because it expects something back – it is unconditional. We must love others to the point where we are willing to lay down our lives for them.

• Serving one another

We are required to serve one another. I have a friend in the USA who is a pastor. I find him to be an amazing example of a person who loves to serve the brethren. He would do anything to make people comfortable. He is one of the few friends I have abroad who would go with me to the airport when I am leaving town. This gracious gentleman takes me to the airport and helps me to carry my luggage. He weighs them for me and helps me to check in. I appreciate what he does to help me so much that I don't grieve when I have to make a sacrifice to honour a speaking engagement in his church.

The spirituality of this man of God may not be seen in profuse speaking in other tongues. He simply wants to serve. Spirituality is often misunderstood to mean doing things that are so abstract that nobody can see their practicality on earth. We are quick to differentiate between things that are spiritual and those that are not. Prayer, reading the Bible, preaching and exercising spiritual gifts are regarded as spiritual things. On the other hand things like serving one another, visiting the sick and the imprisoned and helping others are considered carnal. It is wrong to categorize life this way. Through this wrong categorization, thousands of believers have buried their own gifts and are trying to be like other people.

> *For, brethren, ye have been called unto liberty; only use not liberty for an occasion to the flesh, but by love serve one another.*
>
> *Galatians 5:13*

The Bible says that we should serve one another with love. This is what incarnational leadership is all about – leadership modeled after the example of Christ, which is based on serving others. We are called upon in Galatians 5:13 to serve one another. We have to serve those that are at our level or below our level without feeling inferior. Use your liberty to serve others and not yourself. If you refuse to serve others, God may not curse you but that will be an abuse of liberty. True liberty is channeled into serving others.

Examples Of Service

I. Dorcas – Full Of Good Works.

It is important for us to understand the spirituality of serving one another. A biblical case of serving the brethren is found in the life of Dorcas. She was noted for good works and alms giving. As a gesture of her good deeds she made garments and coats for widows to bless them.

Now there was at Joppa a certain disciple named Tabitha, which by interpretation is called Dorcas: **this woman was full of good works and almsdeeds which she did.**

And it came to pass in those days, that she was sick, and died: whom when they had washed, they laid her in an upper chamber.

And forasmuch as Lydda was nigh to Joppa, and the disciples had heard that Peter was there, they sent unto him two men, desiring him that he would not delay to come to them.

Then Peter arose and went with them. When he was come, they brought him into the upper chamber: and all the widows stood by him weeping, and shewing the coats and garments which Dorcas made, while she was with them.

But Peter put them all forth, and kneeled down, and prayed; and turning him to the body said, Tabitha, arise. And she opened her eyes: and when she saw Peter, she sat up.

And he gave her his hand, and lifted her up, and when he had called the saints and widows, presented her alive.

Acts 9:36-41

Tabitha *(Tebitho)* is the Syriac version of the Hebrew *tsebi*. The Greek word is Dorcas. It means a gazelle or antelope. It is derived from the Hebrew word *sebî* which means beautiful, pleasant and glorious. Dorcas was so named because she had a beautiful nature. It was customary in the east to give the names of beautiful animals to young women. Dorcas was glorious though she was not noted for prayer and spiritual revelation but for service. She was full of good works and almsdeeds. Stephen was noted for being full of the Holy Ghost and power but Dorcas was noted for her services. They were both glorious but in different ways.

This maid of God's people served others with her sewing talent. One day she fell ill and died. The brethren could not allow her to go, so they sent for Peter to come and raise her from the dead. When Peter arrived at the scene where they had laid the dead body of Dorcas, some widows were standing there with the garments and coats she had made for them in their hands. This scene must have moved Peter into earnest prayer for the deceased to be raised. I also believe that the evidence of Dorcas' labour of love in the widows' hands triggered an immediate action from heaven to raise her from the dead – the good works of the woman who clothed widows had to continue. Peter prayed a very simple prayer of two words, "Tabitha, arise" and she was raised from the dead.

Serving others releases miracles into our lives. It is not only prayerful people who get miracles from God; those who serve others obtain favour with God.

Besides serving people at our level and those below us, we have to serve anointings that are above us. It is a common thing these days to find people who don't want to serve under anybody. Everybody wants to be his own boss. Churches are springing up under the leadership of people who are inept in their ability to lead. Businesses are started by people who know nothing about business – they are not interested in the success of the business but in the glory of just being CEOs.

II. Epaphroditus – The Minister.

Epaphroditus, an example of a servant, served Paul until he nearly died. This is an example of how we are supposed to serve the anointings God connects us to.

> Yet I supposed it necessary to send to you Epaphroditus, my brother, and companion in labour, and fellowsoldier, but your messenger, and **he that ministered to my wants.**
> For he longed after you all, and was full of heaviness, because that ye had heard that he had been sick.

For indeed he was sick nigh unto death: but God had mercy on him; and not on him only, but on me also, lest I should have sorrow upon sorrow.

I sent him therefore the more carefully, that, when ye see him again, ye may rejoice, and that I may be the less sorrowful.

Receive him therefore in the Lord with all gladness; and hold such in reputation:

Because for the work of Christ he was nigh unto death, not regarding his life, to supply your lack of service toward me.

Philippians 2:25-30

Paul commended Epaphroditus highly. He was a member of the church in Philippi who was sent to carry relief supplies to Paul in Rome. While in Rome, he fell sick and nearly died. After his recovery Paul sent him back to the Philippians at once. He described his relationship with him to the Philippians in a very captivating manner.

Paul referred to him as a brother – he considered him as belonging to the same spiritual family with himself. The Greek word for "brother" *adelphos*, is connected to the word *delphus* which means the womb. Paul regarded Epaphroditus as a brother from the same womb. They came from the same spiritual source. This is what we are to one another. We must never forget that this bond is stronger than any biological bond we can ever think of. The spirit is always superior to the flesh.

Epaphroditus was a companion in labour – they sweated together. He complemented Paul's giftings and augmented his efforts. He did not work against Paul but rather for him. This companion of Paul made his burden light.

Again, Paul referred to this dear brother of his as a fellow soldier – Paul was a soldier of Christ because Christianity is a battle. Epaphroditus covered Paul in warfare. I believe that he was in constant intercession for the veteran apostle. He brought him food on the battlefield. Each time Paul was weak his fellow soldier was there to provide help. They wrestled with the forces of darkness together and achieved spiritual victories together.

Paul also drew the attention of the Philippians to the fact that Epaphroditus had served as their messenger – he was a delegate, an ambassador and commissioner of Christ. He represented the believers in kingdom matters. Christ sent him with blessings from the Philippians to Paul.

He was also a minister to Paul's needs – this is the supreme test – he was a brother, a companion, a fellow soldier and an apostle of the people but that did not stop him from serving Paul.

This great servant of God was hit by a series of crisis – he was taken ill, he longed for the Philippians and he was full of heaviness when he knew that the Philippians were concerned about his health. Such is the burden of the labour of love.

Just as God raised Dorcas from the dead, He had mercy on Epaphroditus and healed him of his illness. This humble servant of Paul also received other favors from God. The Philippians received him with gladness and he was held in reputation amongst them. Serving does not humiliate us; it does the exact opposite.

The examples of labour of love in the lives of Dorcas and Epaphroditus show distinct marks of the labour of love. The labour of love is what God regards and not just any labour.

The Labour Of Love Under X-Ray

We must have an "X-Ray" of love to know what it is all about. By "X-Ray" here, I am referring to the internal features of the labour of love. You cannot simply look at a person and tell whether his or her labour is a labour of love or not.

I remember that several years ago a young lady was brought into our home by her parents to help us with our household chores. Everything about her looked okay to the naked eye, but I felt funny in my spirit. As I stood there wondering what I should do, I remembered that we needed an item from a shop across the road. Without any good reason I sent her to bring us the item. When she left the door to go I watched her from the window and saw her running. It is good to see a person running to fetch an item but the Holy Ghost told me that she was pretending. I mentioned it to my wife and we sent her away immediately.

A short while after this incident we discovered that she and her family had many problems in their lives that would have given us many challenges in our home. It is commendable for someone to run in the execution of a task, but that is not enough to judge it as labour of love.

An X-Ray of the labour of love will allow us to identify it when we see it. We need to identify it so that we are not misled and also so that we can personally examine ourselves.

When we identify the labour of love, we are able to commend it and reward it appropriately.

Features Of The Labour Of Love

- **No reward is demanded.**

This does not mean that the labour of love is not rewarded. The point I wish to make here is that we should not demand a reward even if it is not available. This does not mean that it is wrong to quote one's price. There is nothing spiritual about allowing the grace of God on your life to be taken for granted. If there is a way you can teach people to be responsible, you have to do so. The apostle Paul taught those who received the ministry of the Word to be responsible to the anointing they benefited from.

We may sometimes however, have to allow ourselves to be defrauded. We should be sensitive about when not to receive anything for our services. It is important to note that you cannot be paid for all the services you render. There are times you would be required to make sacrifices for which no one would reward you.

- **Not for recognition.**

The labour of love is not done for human praise and recognition. Showmanship is not the motive for the labour of love. Eye service is the speciality of hypocrites and unfortunately our churches are choked with them. People do things just to be seen – the spirit of Ananias and Sapphira has consumed them. Others pretend to be humble and do good services but in actual fact they are trying to work themselves into high positions – this is the spirit of Absalom. The Diotrephes spirit which loves to have pre-eminence amongst the brethren graduated from Bible schools with many pastors and leaders. These leaders leave Bible schools and move into churches and try to overshadow everyone else.

Eye service tries to catch the attention of those in authority in order to obtain favour. Paul had a problem of eye service in some of the churches he was overseeing. He urged the believers to be obedient not only in his presence but also in his absence.

Not with eyeservice, as menpleasers; but as the servants of Christ, doing the will of God from the heart;

With good will doing service, as to the Lord, and not
to men:

Ephesians 6:6-7

Believers throng church buildings when a gifted minister is ministering. As soon as the minister leaves and the special atmosphere of the services is withdrawn members recoil into their shells. Most of these members don't go to church because they love God but because they love the touch of a man of God.

- **Holds nothing back.**

The labour of love gives all without holding anything back. The labour of love goes as far as giving its life. **If you are not ready to die for something, you really don't believe in it.** Epaphroditus served the Lord and Paul to the point of death. He risked his life for a cause.

The history of the Church reveals a long blood-stained route on which great messengers of the truth sacrificed their lives. These holy men of old did not seek to save their lives. They took up their crosses and discovered their own Golgothas where they were nailed on those crosses in their own ways.

Death was something they looked forward to. They did not live to live but they lived to die.

The words of Jesus that, he that saves his life will lose it and he that loses his life will save it found real meaning in their practice of religion.

> *Then said Jesus unto his disciples, If any man will come after me, let him deny himself, and take up his cross, and follow me.*
>
> *For whosoever will save his life shall lose it: and*

whosoever will lose his life for my sake shall find it.
Matthew 16:24-25

We must lay our lives on the altar in the love revolution. Our pursuit of God may cost us everything including our lives.

- **The labour of love is not easily offended.**

If you are easily offended when you are serving, your labour is not the labour of love no matter how hard you work. Recently I went to speak for a pastor in his church. He worked very hard to put the meeting together and I congratulated him for that. The meetings were very edifying and powerful.

After the programme I thought all had gone right until another pastor hinted me that my host pastor was angry over a few issues. Firstly, he was accusing me that he mentioned the issue of a conflict between him and another pastor to me and I did not say anything. The truth of the matter however, was that he never raised an issue like that. Either this pastor's mind had led him into erroneous imagination or he was just trying to destroy me.

He also accused me of mobilizing the church members of a pastor who is my son in the Lord in the city to come into the meetings and take over the proceedings with his members. Here again I knew nothing about my son's involvement with the event. I phoned my son to find out how he and his members participated so much in the programme. He told me that my host did not even invite him. He only saw the flyers of the programme and closed down his church and attended our meetings.

In spite of the fact that we had very good meetings, my host pastor conjured up his own speculations. He whined and moaned about things I knew nothing about. When I explained things to him later on, he apologized for his behaviour. This brother missed the point of love. He entangled himself in wounds without any cause. He was supposed to be grateful to me and the participating pastors but he generated non-existent problems. My host wanted something to be grieved about and when he found none, he created them.

When I confronted him with the facts and gave him the evidence that I had nothing to do with the things he was accusing me of, he was very embarrassed. He apologized again and again. I forgave him but it was obvious that, that was not the way to treat a guest preacher.

> *Doth not behave itself unseemly, seeketh not her own, is not easily provoked, thinketh no evil;*
>
> *1 Corinthians 13:5*

Love is not easily provoked. As we work for the Lord and serve His people, it is very easy for people to take us for granted and abuse our gifts. If you are easily provoked, you cannot do the labour of love. Gird up your loins for times of aloneness when people will desert you when you need them most. You will also come face to face with brethren who will use you and dump you when they see other giftings they need. Those you sow seeds of love and labour into are likely to show signs of gross ingratitude and rebellion. The labour of love should not curse people when they fail to return our kind gestures.

• **The labour of love is pure.**

It does not mix sin with work. A preacher must not mix the pleasure of sin with his or her services to the Lord. We cannot preach to sisters and be engaged in immoral acts with them at the same time. It is wrong to use God's people to enrich ourselves. The man of God must not be greedy of filthy lucre. The scriptural standards for a man of God are very high and they require his total consecration.

This is a true saying, If a man desire the office of a bishop, he desireth a good work.

A bishop then must be blameless, the husband of one wife, vigilant, sober, of good behaviour, given to hospitality, apt to teach;

Not given to wine, no striker, not greedy of filthy lucre; but patient, not a brawler, not covetous;

One that ruleth well his own house, having his children in subjection with all gravity;

(For if a man know not how to rule his own house, how shall he take care of the church of God?)

Not a novice, lest being lifted up with pride he fall into the condemnation of the devil.

Moreover he must have a good report of them which are without; lest he fall into reproach and the snare of the devil.

1 Timothy 3:1-7

Workers of the Kingdom must look at these verses again. Some of the words of Paul sound very hard but we cannot lead the flock of God without paying attention to them. We must love the flock we are feeding enough to pay heed to these things. The requirements for ministry are high and we have to be ready to pay the price.

- **The labour of love is willing.**

It does not have to be forced to serve. Too much effort is sometimes applied to get people to do the right things. Reminders have to be served to people to execute their assignments. Promises of reward have to be used as bait to entice several believers to play their role in church. Threats of retribution and curses are employed by dictatorial leaders to force people to do the work of God.

And, behold, the courses of the priests and the Levites,

even they shall be with thee for all the service of the house of God: and there shall be with thee for all manner of workmanship every willing skilful man, for any manner of service: also the princes and all the people will be wholly at thy commandment.

1 Chronicles 28:21

Reference is made to a willing skilful man. It is not enough to be skilful – we must be willing for every manner of service. The word willing in the above verse means to be magnanimous, liberal and generous. A willing heart is the only means through which we can sustain our efforts to obtain results.

- **The labour of love is cheerful.**

It explodes with joy. Many people give their services, lives and material things to God grudgingly. There is no joy in what they do. People sing with sadness and give offerings with offence.

But this I say, He which soweth sparingly shall reap also sparingly; and he which soweth bountifully shall reap also bountifully.

Every man according as he purposeth in his heart, so let him give; not grudgingly, or of necessity: for God loveth a cheerful giver.

2 Corinthians 9:6-7

God loves a cheerful giver. People who give grudgingly are dangerous. When they are offended they may wish to retrieve what they gave. Several years ago I heard of a young man who was offended in a church. Eventually, he decided to leave the church and when he was going he took the set of drums he had purchased for the church away. Such a brother was not walking in love.

- **The labour of love is discerning.**

Don't assume that what you are doing for people is a blessing to them until they tell you so. You have to discern the actual needs of people before you minister to them.

A friend of mine told me an interesting story from the world of politics. A political party in my country presumptuously erected streetlights for a community. They did not know that the living conditions in the community were so bad that the people did rotational sleeping. The bedrooms were so small that occupants of rooms took turns in sleeping. Others spilled into the streets and spread themselves in the dark. The introduction of streetlights disrupted the nocturnal lifestyle of the people and they were angry with the government. During an election they voted against the government for giving them streetlights. One would have thought that it was a good thing to give people streetlights but in this case the people did not appreciate the effort of the government. The labour of love should prayerfully discern the needs of people before it moves to meet them.

Our labour for the Lord must be saturated with the love of God. This is the only way we can please God.

Love is the spice of labour and it is the catalyst of faith. Labour without love cannot satisfy the actual needs of people and faith without love cannot move mountains. Faith works by love – it is energized by love.

Millions of born again believers have concentrated all their efforts in the development of their faith to do exploits. They have failed to realize that faith works by love. Our faith is not moving mountains; neither do the words we speak affect people because our lives are not saturated with love. In the next chapter I wish to show how faith and love are related. They work together to produce results.

CHAPTER 7

FAITH WORKETH BY LOVE

aith and love are connected in their operations. There can be no practice of faith without love. Any attempt to practise faith without love leads to abuse. We would abuse the sick if we attempted to get them healed without love. Jesus was moved with compassion before He healed the sick. He even placed the healing of the sick above the rigid observance of the law of Sabbath.

Faith towards God cannot be active without the love of God. Man in his most pure state cannot measure up to God's standard of holiness and purity. It will require love to be able to trust that God loves us in spite of our state – love believes all things and thinks no evil. We can only believe that we are saved when we know that God loves us. We simply don't qualify for His acts of mercy.

It is exciting to explore the operation of love with faith in every aspect of our Christian walk. Love is everything and we have to realise this otherwise our impact will continue to dwindle. Love is the essential difference between saints and unbelievers.

The Scope Of Faith
We must have absolute faith toward God (faith in God) in every

department of our walk with God. Without love faith is bound to collapse. There are many kinds of faith and all of them operate through love.

⚐ **Faith for Salvation.**

The Bible says that faith works by love. Circumcision and uncircumcision don't determine our salvation – the love of God does.

> For in Jesus Christ neither circumcision availeth any thing,
> nor uncircumcision; but faith which worketh by love.
> *Galatians 5:6*

The kind of faith Paul is talking about in the above verse is saving faith. It is the faith one needs to be reconciled to God. This kind of faith believes in the mercy of God as well as His power to forgive sins and transform a person. One must believe in the power of the love of God to receive this kind of faith in one's heart.

Faith is the ability to believe that when you confess your sins God forgives you. You may not feel forgiven because of shame but that does not change anything.

> If we say that we have no sin, we deceive ourselves, and
> the truth is not in us.
> If we confess our sins, he is faithful and just to forgive
> us our sins, and to cleanse us from all unrighteousness.
> *1 John 1:8-9*

If we confess our sins He is faithful and just to forgive us our sins and to cleanse us from all unrighteousness. Indeed, God goes beyond our expectation of forgiveness for the sins we confess to Him and cleanses us from all other forms of unrighteousness that may be sticking to us at that time and which we may not be aware of.

We are not forgiven and cleansed until we ask and it is obvious that we must love God before we can go to Him in prayer. Love is the force of faith – love pushes faith into God's presence and also moves God to respond to man's faith.

It is only by faith that we can know that our sins are forgiven and that through the substitutionary death of Jesus we are saved.

> *For by grace are ye saved through faith; and that not of*
> *yourselves: it is the gift of God:*
> > *Not of works, lest any man should boast.*
> > > *Ephesians 2:8,9*

Faith is not generated by man's effort. It is the gift of God that is given to us through the love of God. Without the love of God we cannot have faith in Him. He loves us enough to give us the faith to believe in Him. It is like someone giving you money to buy something from him. Faith and love are also connected in the sense that, love and hunger for God are stirred up in our hearts to draw us to God. This happens first and then faith is used to draw forgiveness out of the heart of God.

The unbelieving mind cannot grasp this. He is used to reaching God through dead works that are like filthy rags before God. The unregenerate man believes in a strict observance of ceremonial laws for salvation. To the unbeliever, to say that one is saved is to be presumptuous. He adopts a "wait and see" approach towards the things of God.

☛ Faith for Living.

This is the faith to live the Christian life. Christianity involves taking up one's cross and following Jesus. The cost of discipleship is very high – rejection, mockery and sometimes physical torture. The Christian life could therefore be so tough that one can fall by the way side. If you happen to see giants in the faith falling away you are likely to be afraid for yourself. This fear must be removed from our hearts because our faith is anchored by the love of God. The assurance of God's love for us is what makes us fall in His arms to sustain us. To trust someone, you must be assured of His love.

The Bible says that the just shall live by faith. Faith is the only way by which one can live a life of holiness and obedience to God throughout one's lifetime without going back into sin. A life of holiness is the ultimate goal in the pursuit of God. He is holy and we are to be holy as He is holy. No man has seen God at any time and to be holy like He is holy, we need faith.

> *Behold, his soul which is lifted up is not upright in him:*
> *but the just shall live by his faith.*
> *Habakkuk 2:4*

In I Corinthians 13:5-7 we read that love is not easily provoked, thinks no evil, it does not rejoice in iniquity, bears all things, believes all things, hopes all things and endures all things. Without these elements of love we cannot maintain our fellowship with one another and sustain one another. These qualities of love as a fruit of the Spirit show that God has limitless measures of these and this is why He is able to deliver us from temptation and lift us up any time we fall. God is not easily provoked, He thinks no evil towards us, He bears with us indefinitely, He believes in us because we are His very creation and He endures all our unpredictable characteristics.

> *There hath no temptation taken you but such as is common*
> *to man: but God is faithful, who will not suffer you to be*
> *tempted above that ye are able; but will with the temptation*
> *also make a way to escape, that ye may be able to bear it.*
> *I Corinthians 10:13*

Every temptation you face has a limit. God knows your capacity and He will not allow you to be tempted beyond your ability to survive.

You must have faith in the faithfulness of God that He has adequately prepared you for what you are going through now.

> *Now unto him that is able to keep you from falling, and to present you faultless before the presence of his glory with exceeding joy,*
> *To the only wise God our Saviour, be glory and majesty, dominion and power, both now and ever. Amen.*
> *Jude 1:24,25*

You may look too frail for your present problems but God has provided the means of escape for you. Faith is the only way to embrace God's provision of grace. God is able to keep you from falling. Christianity is not a sprint race, but a marathon and we can only stay focused if we run by faith and not by our sight and feelings.

Sometimes we feel that God is being too hard on us by allowing us to go through certain things. David could have thought that God was too hard on him when He was preparing him to face Goliath. For his training God did not use a stunt object to test his power but a live bear and a live lion.

"But I thought it was just a rehearsal" David may have said. God responded – "the rehearsal of a giant killer is different from that of an ordinary soldier". You are destined to kill giants hence the battles you are facing right now. The reason for your lion and bear is your Goliath. The slaying of Goliath will also usher you into the palace so you should be glad to pay the price. The fight with a lion is a rehearsal for the main event of facing Goliath.

We should have faith in the wisdom of God when He chooses the route of our breakthrough. David went to the school of God's choice. He believed that God loved him too much to allow him to be destroyed by Goliath or the lion and the bear. His faith operated through the love of God for him. He believed God because he knew that God loved him.

☞ Faith for Healing and deliverance.

This kind of faith has to do with believing that your salvation package includes healing and deliverance. The same work of atonement of Jesus on the cross that brought our salvation secured our healing, deliverance from curses and freedom from poverty and misery. He loved us enough to secure our total redemption with a single act of sacrifice on the cross.

> Surely he hath borne our griefs, and carried our sorrows: yet we did esteem him stricken, smitten of God, and afflicted.
>
> But he was wounded for our transgressions, he was bruised for our iniquities: the chastisement of our peace was upon him; and with his stripes we are healed.
>
> All we like sheep have gone astray; we have turned every one to his own way; and the LORD hath laid on him the iniquity of us all.
>
> Isaiah 53:4-6

Jesus was wounded for our transgressions and by His stripes we were healed. The process of crucifixion has made available to us a salvation package of freedom from sin, depression and sickness. Unbelief has multiplied in church circles because people underestimate the love of God. They don't know that God loves them too much to see them afflicted. The coldness of the love of many believers keeps them from the fellowship of the saints where they can be healed and delivered. Worst still is the fact that our love for God has waxed so cold that we would rather go to a doctor for help than go to God for healing. Let us face it – we have a love problem!

> *Bless the LORD, O my soul: and all that is within me, bless his holy name.*
>
> *Bless the LORD, O my soul, and forget not all his benefits:*
>
> *Who forgiveth all thine iniquities; who healeth all thy diseases;*
>
> *Who redeemeth thy life from destruction; who crowneth thee with lovingkindness and tender mercies;*
>
> *Who satisfieth thy mouth with good things; so that thy youth is renewed like the eagle's.*
>
> *Psalm 103:1-5*

Our salvation package in the above verse comprises the forgiveness of our sins and the healing of our diseases. It is very "religious" to attribute sickness to God and glory in it. Nevertheless the Bible is clear on the fact that healing is not something that God adds to forgiveness as an afterthought. Healing is interwoven with the forgiveness of sin.

☞ Faith for God's Provision.

Abraham had the kind of faith that solved the practical problem of lack and want. He told Isaac that the Lord would provide a sacrifice. He called God by the name Jehovah Jireh. God provides our needs because He loves us. In the same way we receive from God by faith because we love Him. We love Him enough to know that He gives us only what is good for us. Even if initially we don't understand God's ways we love Him enough to keep on trusting Him. He does not give us a serpent when we ask Him for fish, neither does He give us a stone instead of bread.

If a son shall ask bread of any of you that is a father, will he give him a stone? or if he ask a fish, will he for a fish give him a serpent?

Or if he shall ask an egg, will he offer him a scorpion?

If ye then, being evil, know how to give good gifts unto your children: how much more shall your heavenly Father give the Holy Spirit to them that ask him?

Luke 11:11-13

Abraham loved God enough to keep trusting Him, though he was instructed to offer his only son Isaac as a sacrifice. He could have doubted God for demanding the only son He gave him but love believes all things – Abraham believed God even when it did not make sense. When Isaac demanded to know where the sacrificial lamb was Abraham answered that God would provide one. The love of God makes him a provider.

And Abraham said, My son, God will provide himself a lamb for a burnt offering: so they went both of them together.

Genesis 22:8

For Abraham to believe that God was going to provide a lamb Himself for the sacrifice was ridiculous. It was a mystery for a man to believe that God was going to provide a lamb on a mountain top. Abraham verbalized what he sensed within him. Until faith begins to speak God simply looks on.

Our words of faith are the raw material for the action products of God's works. Faith without works is dead but faith without words is barren – it produces no fruit.

Jesus taught His disciples to have faith for the provision of their daily needs.

Therefore I say unto you, Take no thought for your life, what ye shall eat, or what ye shall drink; nor yet for your body, what ye shall put on. Is not the life more than meat, and the body than raiment?

Behold the fowls of the air: for they sow not, neither do they reap, nor gather into barns; yet your heavenly Father feedeth them. Are ye not much better than they?

Which of you by taking thought can add one cubit unto his stature?

And why take ye thought for raiment? Consider the lilies of the field, how they grow; they toil not, neither do they spin:

And yet I say unto you, That even Solomon in all his glory was not arrayed like one of these.

Wherefore, if God so clothe the grass of the field, which to day is, and to morrow is cast into the oven, shall he not much more clothe you, O ye of little faith?

Therefore take no thought, saying, What shall we eat? or, What shall we drink? or, Wherewithal shall we be clothed?

(For after all these things do the Gentiles seek:) for your heavenly Father knoweth that ye have need of all these things.

But seek ye first the kingdom of God, and his righteousness; and all these things shall be added unto you.

Take therefore no thought for the morrow: for the morrow shall take thought for the things of itself. Sufficient unto the day is the evil thereof.

Matthew 6:25-34

Jesus in these verses is teaching some common sense faith. He forcefully stated that if God provides food and clothes for birds and plants it must not be difficult to believe that He willingly and

119

lovingly provides for His children. Although God provides our needs we have to ask Him for the provision through prayer and by faith.

Paul said "be careful for nothing; but in everything by prayer and supplication with thanksgiving let your requests be made known unto God" (Philippians 4:6). Millions of believers think that it is not spiritually sound to ask God for material things – they think that it is a sin to pray for money, food, clothing and shelter. This position undermines the goodness of God. It is obvious from Paul's wish for the Philippians that he loved them. We must love people so much that we would do anything in prayer and faith to ensure that their needs are met by God.

The faith to receive provision for daily living is connected to our love for God and the brethren. The life of Gaius in 3 John demonstrates this point. He loved the saints and demonstrated great hospitality towards them. He walked in the truth and John loved him in the truth. The truth in question is not a set of abstract doctrines but practical manifestations of eternal life, such as walking in purity and love.

> *The elder unto the well-beloved Gaius, whom I love in the truth.*
>
> *Beloved, I wish above all things that thou mayest prosper and be in health, even as thy soul prospereth.*
>
> *For I rejoiced greatly, when the brethren came and testified of the truth that is in thee, even as thou walkest in the truth.*
>
> *I have no greater joy than to hear that my children walk in truth.*
>
> *3 John 1-4*

John's language is saturated with love. We don't have to strain our imagination to realize that he loved Gaius in the truth. He wished above all things that Gaius would be in good health and prosper even as his soul prospered. Love propelled John's faith as he prayed for Gaius. Gaius loved the church and did everything possible to promote God's agenda for it. His attitude was different from men like Diotrephes who had no spirit of love in them.

> I wrote unto the church: but Diotrephes, who loveth to have the preeminence among them, receiveth us not.
>
> Wherefore, if I come, I will remember his deeds which he doeth, prating against us with malicious words: and not content therewith, neither doth he himself receive the brethren, and forbiddeth them that would, and casteth them out of the church.
>
> Beloved, follow not that which is evil, but that which is good. He that doeth good is of God: but he that doeth evil hath not seen God.
>
> *3 John 9-11*

Gaius practised true Christianity and John loved him for that. John was definitely comparing Gaius with Diotrephes who was in the assembly with Gaius. Diotrephes did not walk in love – he did not walk in the truth. There can be no greater truth than walking in love. Diotrephes loved pre-eminence among the brethren and was oppressive in his operations. On the contrary Gaius operated in the spirit of love and this triggered the faith of John to ask for the best of all things for him.

If we walk in love it is easier for our prayers of faith to be answered. Walking in love also moves God to answer the prayers others pray for us. I believe that when John wished above all things for the total prosperity of Gaius, God heard his prayer.

☞ Faith For Ministry.

We must have sufficient faith to produce results in ministry. This is what makes ministry easy and the results of ministry abundant. One day the disciples of Jesus failed to cast out a demon from a young man. When Jesus came to the scene of the action later on He cast out the demon with relative ease. His disciples asked Him why they could not cast out the demon earlier on and His reply was that it was because of their unbelief – lack of faith.

> *Then came the disciples to Jesus apart, and said, Why could not we cast him out?*
>
> *And Jesus said unto them, Because of your unbelief: for verily I say unto you, If ye have faith as a grain of mustard seed, ye shall say unto this mountain, Remove hence to yonder place; and it shall remove; and nothing shall be impossible unto you.*
>
> *Howbeit this kind goeth not out but by prayer and fasting.*
>
> *Matthew 17:19-21*

They could not have a successful deliverance session because of their unbelief. Jesus had given them power over demons and the works of the enemy and yet they failed to cast out the demon. Maybe they did not love people enough to fast and pray until they saw their deliverance. Faith works through love and wherever there is love it is easier to release faith. The love of Jesus for people was so strong that His faith was energized to cast out devils.

To have power is not enough. Faith is the catapult that releases power to accomplish results. Love is however, the energizer of faith. Without love faith is limp.

Millions of people are filled with the Holy Ghost and power but they lack the faith to release that power. We must therefore cultivate our faith so that we can obtain great results. Jesus hinted that prayer and fasting are crucial to the development of our faith.

It will require faith to stay in the geographical location of your ministry, if the place is disadvantaged economically and socially. You will need unusual faith to associate with the right people in ministry if their potential is not readily known. You need faith to relate to people based on their future and not their present conditions. Some people have missed great opportunities to develop helpful relationships because they lacked the eye of faith to relate to the future of the people they met instead of their current state of weakness and failure. This kind of faith is directly related to our love for people. Love takes us beyond people's present circumstances. We must love people enough to lay down our lives for them. Faith is a superior sense reserved for spiritual people. Faith and love combine in our lives to release power through us to bless the lives of others.

⮞ Faith for Resurrection.

According to St. Paul faith is required for belief in the resurrection of the dead. You must not be in doubt about this.

> *But I would not have you to be ignorant, brethren, concerning them which are asleep, that ye sorrow not, even as others which have no hope.*
>
> *For if we believe that Jesus died and rose again, even so them also which sleep in Jesus will God bring with him.*
>
> *For this we say unto you by the word of the Lord, that we which are alive and remain unto the coming of the Lord shall not prevent them which are asleep.*
>
> *For the Lord himself shall descend from heaven with a shout, with the voice of the archangel, and with the trump of God: and the dead in Christ shall rise first:*
>
> *Then we which are alive and remain shall be caught*

up together with them in the clouds, to meet the Lord in the air: and so shall we ever be with the Lord.
Wherefore comfort one another with these words.
1 Thessalonians 4:13-18

How can the dead be raised after their bodies have returned to the dust from which they were taken? If a wild beast devours a person and his or her body parts are scattered in several directions how will this person be raised as one whole person? Faith and hope are the only means by which we can attain this superior level of existence that makes the resurrection real.

We have to love the appearing of the Lord Jesus to be partakers of the resurrection.

> *Henceforth there is laid up for me a crown of righteousness, which the Lord, the righteous judge, shall give me at that day: and not to me only, but unto all them also that love his appearing.*
> *2 Timothy 4:8*

Faith for the resurrection is connected to our love for the appearing of the Lord Jesus. We are longing to see the Lord face to face. This longing generates faith in our hearts and propels us to do the things that will hasten the coming of the Lord.

Jesus had faith in the Father to raise Him from the dead and He promised the believers resurrection from the dead.

> *Therefore doth my Father love me, because I lay down my life, that I might take it again.*
> *No man taketh it from me, but I lay it down of myself. I have power to lay it down, and I have power to take it again. This commandment have I received of my Father.*
> *John 10:17,18*

Jesus believed that He had the power to lay down His life and take it back. He was confident that death could not take Him captive. To die knowing that you would rise again is not an act of religious routine. It takes absolute faith in God to do that. Millions of people have been deserted by their best friends and relatives after their death. Those who pretended to love them most neglected their families and destroyed their legacy on earth after their death. Jesus knew that the Father loved Him and would not forsake Him.

> And this is the Father's will which hath sent me, that of all which he hath given me I should lose nothing, but should raise it up again at the last day.
>
> And this is the will of him that sent me, that every one which seeth the Son, and believeth on him, may have everlasting life: and I will raise him up at the last day.
>
> No man can come to me, except the Father which hath sent me draw him: and I will raise him up at the last day
>
> Whoso eateth my flesh, and drinketh my blood, hath eternal life; and I will raise him up at the last day.
>
> *John 6:39,40,44,54*

It is a high expression of faith to believe that Jesus will raise us up on the last day. If we love Jesus we will not doubt Him. We love Him enough to believe Him. If He can give us eternal life – the God kind of life, then He can raise us from the dead. To be born again involves the death of the old man and the raising of a new man in us. The continuous flow of healing and other benefits of the Lord in our lives prove that He will raise us up on the last day.

⚑ Faith for Eternal Judgement.

The early apostles lived in the hope of the resurrection and eternal reward. They did not live with the fear of judgement and condemnation. They had faith and boldness that they would not be condemned in the sight of God. They experienced the love of God and they loved Him so much that they did not doubt their eternal justification. Perfect love casts out fear.

> *Herein is our love made perfect, that we may have boldness in the day of judgment: because as he is, so are we in this world.*
>
> *There is no fear in love; but perfect love casteth out fear: because fear hath torment. He that feareth is not made perfect in love.*
>
> *1 John 4:17-18*

There is no doubt that faith and love are inseparable. The operation of faith is at a low point in our time because of the diminished dimension of love in the Church. Our love for the world has suffocated our love for God and the eternal realm. Carnality has glued the feet of thousands of believers to the systems of the world. We need a sweeping love revolution to tear us away from the force of cohesion that binds us to the cosmos. Love not the world, neither the things that are in the world.

> *Love not the world, neither the things that are in the world. If any man love the world, the love of the Father is not in him.*
>
> *For all that is in the world, the lust of the flesh, and the lust of the eyes, and the pride of life, is not of the Father, but is of the world.*
>
> *And the world passeth away, and the lust thereof: but he that doeth the will of God abideth for ever.*
>
> *1 John 2:15-17*

The love revolution must take place now. We must overthrow the systems of the world from the Church. The lust of the flesh, the lust of the eyes and the pride of life must be banished from the Church.

The apostle Paul was bold about the fact that he was going to be crowned by God. He knew that he was a heavenly laureate. Paul did not hide his faith and confidence in the truth that he was not going to be disqualified by God. He knew in whom he had believed and knew that a crown awaited him.

> *For the which cause I also suffer these things: nevertheless I am not ashamed: for I know whom I have believed, and am persuaded that he is able to keep that which I have committed unto him against that day.*
> *2 Timothy 1:12*

By faith Paul fought a good fight and finished his course. He kept the faith and he had every good reason to expect a crown of righteousness.

> *I have fought a good fight, I have finished my course, I have kept the faith:*
> *Henceforth there is laid up for me a crown of righteousness, which the Lord, the righteous judge, shall give me at that day: and not to me only, but unto all them also that love his appearing.*
> *2 Timothy 4:7-8*

Paul was not proud when he said that a crown of righteousness was awaiting him. His confession was an expression of faith that was predicated on the love of God and not his own works of righteousness. Religious people get offended when Christians appear very sure that they are going to heaven. They think that these believers are blaspheming because only God should know who qualifies for eternal life. But the truth is that the believer has the blueprint of the Word of God. Through this Word and the inner witness of the Holy Spirit the believer knows what the future holds for him or her. His disposition is an assurance of faith.

You must be convinced that you will not be condemned at the Judgment Seat of Christ. The unsaved are not sure of their fate but the believer is persuaded by faith that he does not stand condemned before God.

> *There is therefore now no condemnation to them which are in Christ Jesus, who walk not after the flesh, but after the Spirit.*
> *For the law of the Spirit of life in Christ Jesus hath made me free from the law of sin and death.*
> *Romans 8:1,2*

The scope of our faith stretches from the time of our new birth to the judgement seat of Christ. This makes faith an indispensable part of your life. We must therefore seek to develop our faith and release it for maximum results. We must know how faith works and the accomplishments it achieves.

The sum total of how faith works and its accomplishments is what I term the workability of faith. One of the keys for the workability of faith is the energizing effect of love.

Understanding the principles by which faith operates makes it easy to operate in faith. These principles are of universal application. The key principle for operating faith in God is love. Every believer can apply the key of love and obtain great results.

We have discovered that love is the supernatural factor that empowers faith to produce results. Besides this, love is a weapon through which conquest is achieved in all the battles the believer encounters. People often wrongly associate love with weakness. They think that if they walk in the love of God they would be losers in a world that is rife with competition and antagonism. The fear of being a victim of the wickedness and selfishness of men has dissuaded many from walking in the love of God.

CHAPTER 8

CONQUEST BY LOVE

*T*he desire for conquest and supremacy is one of the strongest instincts of humankind. Conquest is a gift from God. He makes us to triumph in Christ Jesus in every place. God told Joshua that every place that the soles of his feet would touch was given to him to possess. Jesus commanded His disciples to go into all nations and make disciples of them – to disciple the nations, is to take charge of the destinies of people. Conquest is a good thing – it is a blessing. In our pursuit of conquest and dominion however, we should be wary of certain disturbing trends in the Church.

The word of faith movement and the prophetic emphasis of our time have precipitated an unhealthy trend of competition amongst us, with people trying to outdo one another using very carnal methods. It does not matter to people these days who they hurt in the process of getting what they want. Materialism and power struggles have turned many churches into battlefields. Homes have been ripped apart as family members surrender to selfishness in their quest for supremacy.

Anointings are operating below capacity and the witness of the Church is compromised by our carnal instincts. Preachers

betray one another to the media. They do everything they can to destroy the reputation of preachers who are doing well in the ministry. We want to be featured in magazines, dine with politicians and capture the inquisitive lenses of television cameras. Spiritual gifts are emphasized in a typical "Corinthians fashion" – we do nothing to check carnality in the exercising of our gifts. Gospel musicians pay no attention to their spiritual lives. All they want is the limelight. Love has departed from the corridors of the Church.

The ambition of pastors for success and breakthrough has made it difficult for us to walk in love. The rules of decency and the golden rule to love your neighbour as yourself are completely disregarded as we try to build our human kingdoms and empires. We must not succeed at the expense of people's lives. Our anointings must not be used to oppress God's people but to liberate them.

In February, 2006, I was ministering in Amsterdam at my annual meetings dubbed "Strategic Ambushment". One night the anointing was so strong that one could almost call it a tangible anointing. I was so heavy with the anointing and I spoke under a strong inspiration. The sick were healed and the prophetic flow was amazing. **At a certain point I asked the Lord in my spirit why Elisha in the Bible was more anointed than the preacher of today. God's answer was very sharp "Elisha had no church."** This answer startled me. Elisha was more anointed than us because he had no church. Elisha raised the dead and cleansed the leper because he was not encumbered with the problems of a church.

The pastor of a church is so easily distracted from prayer and the Word of God by the burden of the church. Administrative demands, counselling and the financial pressures of church work take a lot of the pastor's time. The pastor is sometimes compelled by his detractors in the church to employ political schemes to survive the undermining efforts of disloyal people. Elisha had no church. He provided leadership for the school of the prophets but he was not the Presiding Bishop or Senior Pastor of a church who had to do everything possible to prevent his ministry from being snatched away by associate pastors. He spoke the Word of God without the fear of losing congregation members. Elisha went where God sent him – he had no church to pin him down to a place. Elisha had no church so he operated beyond the church walls. He even had influence on Syria.

Elisha had no church so it was easier for him to operate in love. The challenges of a pastor in church can make it difficult for him to operate in love. Ungrateful members and grieved souls in the church pews can rob a pastor of the spirit of agape. We can pastor churches and still live as though we did not pastor any. We do this by not trying to hold on to everything – the power, the money and the glory. Don't abuse the members of the church by using them to satisfy your lusts.

Love must pervade every aspect of our lives. We can conquer with love. We must be different from the world. Some nations of the world are involved in active programmes to develop weapons of mass destruction in an attempt to conquer other nations.

In the current nuclear arms race, communist North Korea shocked the world by announcing on Monday, 9th October, 2006 that it had conducted its first-ever nuclear test. The nation's leader Kim Jong-Il has resisted any attempts by the United States of America and the Western World to suppress North Korea's zest to acquire nuclear power. Closely following the heels of Kim Jong-Il is the Iranian President, Mahmoud Ahmadinejad, who has vowed not to discontinue his Uranium enrichment programme. He has threatened repeatedly that Israel will disappear. These and many other examples indicate strongly that the nations of the world believe they can conquer the world by violence.

The history of humankind however proves otherwise. Some major victories have been won without weapons and conquests have been attained without the carnage of war. One of the means through which conquests have been attained in history is by the perverted form of love.

Delilah overpowered the great Samson with a sweet tongue. She penetrated the weakness of Samson with perverted love and the man who could not be captured by one thousand men was rendered powerless by the deceptive wiles of a single woman. Pretentious love disarmed Samson. Lust deflated him and the amorous overtures of a woman from the other side of the world (hell) destroyed the man God had given unusual strength (Judges 16:4-21).

Judas betrayed Jesus with a kiss. The betrayer used a kiss to isolate Jesus from the people He was standing with. This historic kiss carried mischievous laser precision – it left the captors of Jesus in no doubt about the one they wanted to arrest.

> *Now he that betrayed him gave them a sign, saying, Whomsoever I shall kiss, that same is he: hold him fast.*
> *Matthew 26:48*

A pretentious kiss delivered the Messiah into the hands of sinners. Judas Iscariot employed the time-tested secret of "love" to betray the originator and embodiment of divine love.

The animal kingdom portrays the power of the perverted form of love in the mating habit of the female praying mantis. The mantis is famous for its almost human mating habits. The interesting feature of this mating habit is however, that when the male and female are done mating, the female eats the male. The female conquers and devours the male with the power of corrupted love.

Thousands of strong men have been slain in history by women. Men have similarly employed the corrupted version of love to subdue powerful women. Women who possess vast amounts of money and power have had their empires crushed by simply falling into the arms of mischievous men.

People have used the perverted forms of love to conquer their opponents and possess territories. If these perverted forms of love could do exploits then the power of uncorrupted love should be harnessed by the Church.

Nations are engaged in the nuclear arms race in their bid to gain supremacy over one another. Dictators and terrorists are using every means within their power to acquire weapons of mass destruction. The Church has drifted along the lines of the world. We try to fight our battles with the weapons of the flesh. We employ vicious tactics to destroy one another. **We fail to grasp the fact that there is only one weapon which wins a battle without destroying any life and that weapon is love.** Paradoxically, the Church of today has neglected its greatest and strongest weapon, which is love.

The blood of Jesus Christ is the weapon God employed to disarm Satan and make an open show of Him. We must understand that the blood of Jesus and His love are inseparable.

The love of Jesus is the active ingredient of His blood.

The Overcoming Blood

We know that the saints overcome the enemy by the blood of the lamb. The blood of Jesus is a weapon of warfare. What we do not understand is that it is not just the blood that overcomes but the spirit behind the blood – the spirit of love. Many people have shed their blood in battle for their people but the blood did not save the people. The reason is that the blood of these human beings was Adamic blood which cannot save. Again the blood of these men was not shed because of perfect love but because of selfish motives.

> *And they overcame him by the blood of the Lamb, and by the word of their testimony; and they loved not their lives unto the death.*
>
> Revelation 12:11

The reason why we overcome by the blood of Jesus is because it is saturated with so much love that it cleanses the vilest offender and delivers the most oppressed. The blood of Jesus speaks better things than the blood of Abel.

> *And he said, What hast thou done? the voice of thy brother's blood crieth unto me from the ground.*
>
> *And now art thou cursed from the earth, which hath opened her mouth to receive thy brother's blood from thy hand;*
>
> Genesis 4:10-11

The blood of Abel cried unto God and what followed was a curse on his assailant – Cain. The blood of Abel called for vengeance otherwise God could have blessed Cain instead of cursing him and the ground. It is appropriate to mention that when Stephen was stoned he asked for God's forgiveness for his assailants – he asked God not to lay their sin to their charge (Acts 7:60). The result of his prayer was that Paul, who was the supervisor of Stephen's death, received grace later on to become an apostle.

The blood of Jesus speaks better things than the blood of Abel. It speaks about love and forgiveness. On the cross of Calvary Jesus asked the Father to forgive those who crucified Him because they did not know what they were doing.

And to Jesus the mediator of the new covenant, and to the blood of sprinkling, that speaketh better things than that of Abel.

Hebrews 12:24

Abel did not die voluntarily – he was murdered. Jesus laid down His life because of His love for humanity. Abel's blood was human blood, which was laced with sin. Even if he laid down his life voluntarily, it could not have saved anyone. The blood of Jesus is pure and without sin. Motivated by the strongest love the world has ever seen, He shed His blood to overcome sin, sickness and death.

Greater love hath no man than this, that a man lay down his life for his friends.

John 15:13

With love Jesus overcame sin, death and the grave. No weapon of warfare can overcome death and the grave. Great generals and statesmen in history have perished without resurrection. They could not overcome the force of the grave. These men did not possess enough love to overcome death and the grave.

Napoleon Bonaparte, the French emperor who could be compared only with Julius Caesar and Alexander the Great perished on May 5, 1821. He is suspected to have died either by poisoning or stomach cancer on the god-forsaken Island of St. Helena, in the South Atlantic.

On 15th March, 44BC, Julius Caesar, the Roman general and political leader, died from twenty three wounds inflicted on him by his trusted servants. The second of the wounds in the breast proved to be the most lethal.

Alexander the great, king of Macedonia, conqueror of much of Asia, died on June 10, 323 BC, at the age of 33. He is believed to have died either of poisoning or a raging fever. His death dealt a lethal blow to the aspirations of his people but it could not give them salvation because he was also human and needed to be saved.

The death of Jesus is different from the death of these great men because His death led to the salvation of man. His blood was different from their blood because it spoke about forgiveness. The great conquerors of the world speak hatred and practice brutality. The love of Jesus makes His blood different and His death superior.

Overcome Evil With Good

There is an ongoing battle between good and evil, light and darkness. We are surrounded by hostile forces whose aim is to destroy what God is doing in our lives. Evil doers invade our lives daily with temptations that provoke us to walk in unforgiveness and selfishness. There is often a great temptation to repay evil for evil. As people try to defraud us and use worldly wisdom to gain advantage over us, we must be careful not to descend to their level of carnality. Arguments don't win favour, neither do weapons secure victories.

> Recompense to no man evil for evil. Provide things honest in the sight of all men.
>
> If it be possible, as much as lieth in you, live peaceably with all men.
>
> Dearly beloved, avenge not yourselves, but rather give place unto wrath: for it is written, Vengeance is mine; I will repay, saith the Lord.
>
> Therefore if thine enemy hunger, feed him; if he thirst, give him drink: for in so doing thou shalt heap coals of fire on his head.
>
> Be not overcome of evil, but overcome evil with good.
>
> Romans 12:17-21

The command here is to overcome evil with good. Vengeance is the Lord's. Don't destroy other people's reputations in an attempt to protect yours. Feed your enemies and recompense no man evil for evil. The words of the apostle Paul in the above verses of scripture present a new kind of philosophy. They seem to be screaming at our generation that we are heading the wrong way. These words are revolutionary. They oppose our sense of logic and contradict what our present breed of leaders is trying to teach us. The leaders of our time want to succeed and they would sacrifice and destroy anybody to do so.

Jesus showed the way in the love revolution. He did not fight those that came against Him carrying swords, with a sword. At His betrayal Peter drew out his sword and with the precision of a veteran swordsman he slashed off the ear of Malchus, the servant of the High Priest who was amongst those that had come to capture Jesus (John 18:10).

Jesus reached out and healed Malchus before He proceeded to His trial (Luke 22:51). He told Peter that all who draw the sword perish by the sword.

> *Then said Jesus unto him, Put up again thy sword into his place: for all they that take the sword shall perish with the sword.*
>
> *Matthew 26:52*

Jesus is showing us the more excellent way – the way of love. In His teachings, our savior presented God's law in a manner that startled the teachers of the day. He shifted the definition of godliness from external show to inner virtue. The eternal light of the world positioned love at the centre of godliness and precipitated a paradigm shift that threatened the impotent piety of the Pharisees. The Pharisees disassociated love from godliness but Jesus predicated godliness on love and taught that love was indeed the summation of the law. The ancient giver of the law revolutionized the interpretation of the written law. He raised the standards but at the same time made the fulfillment of the law possible. He did this by teaching on the power of the Holy Spirit, the forgiving heart of God, the unity of the body of Christ and empowerment through the Word of God.

Revolutionary Laws

Every revolution is characterized by new laws. A revolution is defined as a sudden and drastic change. It is a sudden turn around. Jesus presented a revolutionized version of the Law of Moses when He walked on earth. He did not break the law but He ushered us into its fullness and fulfillment. He emphasized the spirit of the law whereas the teachers of the law presented its letter.

The love revolution is on-going. I must however, state that it is not new. It is only being rediscovered. The Lord Jesus started this revolution thousands of years ago. Jesus introduced a radical and complete change in what spiritual life was all about. He frequently brought up some of the teachings and beliefs of the leaders of the day, and then went on to establish the new way of looking at the truth of God's word. He did not change the word of God but the way of looking at it.

☞ Murder Redefined.

Jesus introduced His revolutionary concepts with the following words - "Ye have heard that it was said by them of old time," (Matthew 5:21).

> *Ye have heard that it was said by them of old time, Thou shalt not kill; and whosoever shall kill shall be in danger of the judgment:*

139

But I say unto you, That whosoever is angry with his brother without a cause shall be in danger of the judgment: and whosoever shall say to his brother, Raca, shall be in danger of the council: but whosoever shall say, Thou fool, shall be in danger of hell fire.

Therefore if thou bring thy gift to the altar, and there rememberest that thy brother hath ought against thee;

Leave there thy gift before the altar, and go thy way; first be reconciled to thy brother, and then come and offer thy gift.

Agree with thine adversary quickly, whiles thou art in the way with him; lest at any time the adversary deliver thee to the judge, and the judge deliver thee to the officer, and thou be cast into prison.

Verily I say unto thee, Thou shalt by no means come out thence, till thou hast paid the uttermost farthing.
Matthew 5:21-26

He redefined murder by saying that murder is more than killing someone physically. Jesus said that if one is angry with one's neighbor and calls him a fool, one is in danger of hell fire. The master revolutionary said that if a person brought a sacrifice to the altar and remembered that someone had a grudge against him, he had to go back and make peace before he came to offer the sacrifice. It is amazing how people lift up their hands in church to worship God and others carry powerful microphones to preach with massive amounts of anger and bitterness in them. Hatred is classified as murder in the love revolution.

The apostle John said that anybody who hates his brother is a murderer.

We know that we have passed from death unto life, because we love the brethren. He that loveth not his brother abideth in death.

Whosoever hateth his brother is a murderer: and ye know that no murderer hath eternal life abiding in him.
1 John 3:14-15

He that does not love his brother abides in death. A person who hates his brother is a murderer and has no eternal life in him. Unforgiveness, bitterness, unresolved issues and other related things are all to be classified under murder. It is a fact that people who go to the altar often are most guilty of the sins of the heart. While they walk in hatred and bitterness they hide behind prayer and spiritual activities.

Ahithophel, the advisor of King David, was called to join Absalom's rebellion at a time when he was offering a sacrifice.

*And Absalom sent for Ahithophel the Gilonite, David's counsellor, from his city, even from Giloh, **while he offered sacrifices**. And the conspiracy was strong; for the people increased continually with Absalom.*
2 Samuel 15:12

Ahithophel was busy offering sacrifices when Absalom, David's son, invited him to join his camp. I believe that Ahithophel had some unresolved issues with the king. The invitation of Absalom provided him the perfect opportunity to hit back at David. Bitter people are unstable. They have no love in their hearts and this affects their loyalty and commitment to their families and friends. Ahithophel joined a rebellion and in no time lives were lost including that of Absalom. He did not love the king enough to stay out of the mischievous enterprises of Absalom and this led to the death of the king's son. Hatred can lead to murder. Anger is the prelude to murder and the earlier we treated them as the same thing the better.

☞ A New Look At Adultery And Divorce.

Adultery is traditionally defined as illicit sex between a married person and a single person or another married person. Couples are quick to conclude that they are not cheating on their spouses, simply because they have not been engaged in physical adultery.

Jesus however, raised the moral standard. The people of old defined adultery a certain way but the "Logos Word" dwelling among men defined it another way. The teachers of the word understood adultery as physical activity one engaged in. The "personified Word" thought otherwise. He taught the people that adultery is not only a bodily thing but also a heart thing. He was emphatic about the fact that anybody who looks at a woman to lust after her commits adultery with her in his heart.

A new look at adultery was established by the giver of the law.

> *Ye have heard that it was said by them of old time, Thou shalt not commit adultery:*
>
> *But I say unto you, That whosoever looketh on a woman to lust after her hath committed adultery with her already in his heart.*
>
> *And if thy right eye offend thee, pluck it out, and cast it from thee: for it is profitable for thee that one of thy members should perish, and not that thy whole body should be cast into hell.*
>
> *And if thy right hand offend thee, cut it off, and cast it from thee: for it is profitable for thee that one of thy members should perish, and not that thy whole body should be cast into hell.*
>
> *It hath been said, Whosoever shall put away his wife, let him give her a writing of divorcement:*
>
> *But I say unto you, That whosoever shall put away his wife, saving for the cause of fornication, causeth her*

142

to commit adultery: and whosoever shall marry her that is divorced committeth adultery.

Matthew 5:27-32

Jesus taught His hearers to be aggressive in their bid to live right. Nothing was to stop them from living right. He urged them to pluck out their right eyes and cut off their right hands if that was the only way they could avoid hell fire. I believe that the eye is the eye of lust for adultery and the hands are the instruments of the body we employ for immoral acts.

Jesus is admonishing us to do everything possible to subdue any sin-prone part of our bodies and lives. He extended fornication beyond a physical act – looking at a woman lustfully is judged to be an act of fornication.

The inspirer and author of the Holy Scriptures also threw more light on the issue of divorce. He said that in the days of old one was permitted to write a bill of divorcement and send his wife away. In the new day of love however, we are not permitted to do so except on the grounds of fornication. Even there the power of forgiveness can let an act of adultery receive forgiveness instead of divorce. There is great danger in divorcing a spouse – the person is tempted to commit adultery. Other parts of the scriptures teach that woe be to him that causes offences to come (Matthew 18:7). Giving a writing of divorcement is not enough to give us peace about divorce. A higher law of love must make us more committed to a marriage than scriptural exceptions.

It is clear that Jesus raised the standards rather than lowered them. Murder was not just physical killing – hatred was considered to be murder. Adultery was no longer just physical contact but an issue of the heart. In the same way divorce was to be interpreted beyond the permission of the law to give a bill of divorcement. The law of the Spirit being love and forgiveness was to take over from the letter of the law being the presentation of a bill of divorcement.

I am not a specialist on matters of divorce but it is obvious from the saying of Jesus above that His moral standards for divorce and adultery are higher than the Old Testament requirements.

The Jewish doctors gave great liberties and license in the matters of divorce. The school of Hillel gave much license – a man could divorce his wife if she no longer pleased him or if he found another woman prettier than her. The school of Shammai however, permitted divorce only on the grounds of adultery. Jesus however, sought to entrench a law of love that was higher than either of these. By saying that he who put away a wife caused her to commit adultery He was saying something new, which was above the Shammai school of thought. Nobody who loves a spouse wants to give her a bill of divorcement and lead her into adultery. Jesus was therefore saying that if one loves one's spouse with true agape love and can forgive him or her for committing adultery it is better.

We are under no compulsion to divorce a spouse on the grounds of adultery if it is possible for the offending party to repent and be forgiven. This is however, no license to hurt spouses in marriage because they don't have to divorce. The truth of the matter is that sometimes the offended parties are hurt beyond what they can handle. As much as they would have wished to continue a relationship the pain makes it impossible to do so. Agape love must make us love our spouses without doing the things that hurt them. It must also make us love our spouses without using the least excuse to jump out of relationships.

Divorce is a very debatable subject and we have to approach it with a lot of caution. The people who go through divorce suffer a lot of pain and we must not add to their pain by standing in judgment against them. We have to demonstrate a lot of love towards people who are caught in the trap of divorce.

☙ False Swearing.

The men of old permitted some form of making vows or swearing oaths if only the ones who made them knew that they would not default in their delivery. Jesus discouraged the people from swearing altogether. In the love revolution we are admonished to keep our words simple. Our yea should be yea and our nay, nay. We should not be pressurized to add more to what we want to tell God.

> *Again, ye have heard that it hath been said by them of old time, Thou shalt not forswear thyself, but shalt perform unto the Lord thine oaths:*
>
> *But I say unto you, Swear not at all; neither by heaven; for it is God's throne:*
>
> *Nor by the earth; for it is his footstool: neither by Jerusalem; for it is the city of the great King.*
>
> *Neither shalt thou swear by thy head, because thou canst not make one hair white or black.*
>
> *But let your communication be, Yea, yea; Nay, nay: for whatsoever is more than these cometh of evil.*
>
> *Matthew 5:33-37*

To forswear is to make false vows or swear falsely. We are not to make vows by swearing by heaven, earth, Jerusalem or our heads. Vows are very sensitive in nature. When they are made to God they must be fulfilled otherwise we would be mocking God.

If we make the vows to people, they receive them whole-heartedly. Failure to deliver on our vows can destroy the life of a human being we vowed to. Vows and promises are made to human hearts and not to their bones. When we break them we literally destroy lives. This is what makes the vows we make to one another during weddings very sensitive. Marriage vows are made in the presence of people and in God's sight. God is involved with the vows;

indeed He is the actual officiator of the marriage. To break the vow is therefore a serious matter to God. We must fulfill the vows we make to God and before God. In the love revolution Jesus said that we should not vow at all.

The love revolution seeks to banish hurt and eradicate our tendency to hurt one another and offend God. If we truly love one another we would treat our word so sacredly that we would not need a vow to fulfill it. When we speak under the impulse of love, swearing becomes unnecessary. Jesus was teaching His hearers not to hide behind vows when they knew they would not fulfill what they were promising to do.

An Eye For An Eye.

Normal, natural law says an eye for an eye and a tooth for a tooth. The law of retaliation was what the people had been practising. In this law the offender was required to suffer the same pain he or she had committed. Some people carried this law to the extreme and retribution became disproportionate to the offence.

> *Ye have heard that it hath been said, An eye for an eye, and a tooth for a tooth:*
> *But I say unto you, That ye resist not evil: but whosoever shall smite thee on thy right cheek, turn to him the other also.*
> *And if any man will sue thee at the law, and take away thy coat, let him have thy cloke also.*
> *And whosoever shall compel thee to go a mile, go with him twain.*
> *Give to him that asketh thee, and from him that would borrow of thee turn not thou away.*
> *Matthew 5:38-42*

Jesus, the man who suffered the greatest injustice the world has ever known, advocated a new law which forbade retaliation. The love revolution initiated by Jesus requires us to offer the left cheek when the right one is smitten. If anyone took us to court and took away our coat (under garment) we should give them our cloak (our garment) also. In life there are people who would demand more labour from us than they ought to. If such people compel us to go one mile and we know that going two miles will glorify God we should do so.

It is obvious that the above philosophy flies in the face of our belief system. We are taught to resist any form of wrongdoing people dish out to us. In the love revolution we are expected to suffer wrong without retaliation. Church life can be very bumpy with people ramming into us every now and then. If one wants to react to all the things that are thrown at one daily, one cannot walk in love.

Concerning Your Enemies.

At individual, ethnic, national and international levels people are indoctrinated to hate their enemies. The tension in the world, in our churches and in our homes is on the increase. Hearts are overflowing with anger and people's hands cannot wait to execute vengeance. During Jesus' earthly walk the situation was no different. The Jews and the Samaritans were at one another's throats. The Pharisees and Sadducees used religion as the excuse to continue their hostilities against one another.

> *Ye have heard that it hath been said, Thou shalt love thy neighbour, and hate thine enemy.*
> *But I say unto you, Love your enemies, bless them that curse you, do good to them that hate you, and pray for them which despitefully use you, and persecute you;*
> *That ye may be the children of your Father which is in heaven: for he maketh his sun to rise on the evil and on the*

good, and sendeth rain on the just and on the unjust.

For if ye love them which love you, what reward have ye? Do not even the publicans the same?

And if ye salute your brethren only, what do ye more than others? do not even the publicans so?

Be ye therefore perfect, even as your Father which is in heaven is perfect.

Matthew 5:43-48

Jesus taught His disciples to love their enemies and bless those who curse them. They were to do good to those that hated them and pray for those who persecuted them. If we love only those who love us, we are no different from the wicked. It is difficult to love people who hate you. It is also difficult to pray for them and yet that is what the love revolution requires of us.

Jesus taught His disciples the most powerful weapon of conquest. His understanding of life also reveals what true life is all about. As He walked on the face of the earth, the Lord of the universe and the God of all wisdom transcended the existing laws that bordered on selfishness. Motivated by love, He turned everything upside down.

If you don't know what true life is, you will not know how to live it.

If you don't know that true life is living for others and not yourself, you will waste all your efforts on selfish ventures. A warped understanding of victory will make you employ carnal means just to appear victorious. It is important that we identify what true conquest is. It is crucial to know that true life is not just physical existence.

A new dispensation is dawning on us. Love is taking over from hatred. The time has arrived when we will not destroy one another but co-habit in peace and love. I see families coming together. God is calling His people up to His Holy Mountain where there is no chaos but the spirit of agape. The world is about to witness an amazing dispensation of love in the Church. This flow of love in God's household will be a great tool of evangelism in the last days. By our love, the world will know that we know God.

CHAPTER 9

THE DISPENSATION OF LOVE

The word dispensation comes from the Greek word *oikonomia* which means management, economy, a disposition of affairs entrusted to one or a stewardship. The Greek word is taken from two words *oikos* meaning a house and *nomos* meaning a law.

It means the method or scheme according to which God carries out His purposes towards a man or people (house), through the instrument of a specific revelation (law). Dispensation is also defined as an era of time during which man is tested with respect to obedience in a definite area of revelation of God's will. Seven such dispensations are recognized by many premillennialists. Other premillennialists speak of only three or four. Those who hold to seven dispensations list them as follows: innocence, conscience, human government, promise, law, grace and the kingdom.

In this chapter I am using the word dispensation in a liberal way to mean the act of dispensing love to believers and other people by God, during a special season of the manifestation of grace. The dispensation of love is a scheme according to which God brings His people together in love for the fulfillment of His eternal purposes. The Church is maturing into a dispensation of love. A new wave of love is finding its way into the Church.

The dispensation of love will climax in the righteous rule of Christ on earth. Isaiah had a perfect vision of the state of peace during the reign of the Messiah. He presented a perfect picture where people will not hurt nor destroy one another on the holy mountain of God.

> *The wolf also shall dwell with the lamb, and the leopard shall lie down with the kid; and the calf and the young lion and the fatling together; and a little child shall lead them.*
>
> *And the cow and the bear shall feed; their young ones shall lie down together: and the lion shall eat straw like the ox.*
>
> *And the sucking child shall play on the hole of the asp, and the weaned child shall put his hand on the cockatrice' den.*
>
> *They shall not hurt nor destroy in all my holy mountain: for the earth shall be full of the knowledge of the LORD, as the waters cover the sea.*
>
> *Isaiah 11:6-9*

We see in these verses the beautiful assembling of images that portray the great peace and tranquility of the kingdom of the Messiah. The prophet, borrowing his imagery from the animal kingdom shows how gentiles and Jews and peoples from all backgrounds will dwell together in love. None shall hurt another in all the holy mountain of God – Zion the seat of the Messiah's government. From this holy mountain love will flow to every corner of the earth. This is the climax of the operation of the love of God. Like any other heavenly or Kingdom blessing, the love of God will be experienced by the Church in a strong way before the end of time.

Glimpses of the kingdom of the Messiah will unfold before our eyes. As we look into the perfect picture we will be changed into the same from glory to glory. Some parts of the Body of Christ are experiencing the coming supernatural love already. The vast majority of believers don't know this kind of love, but it is steadily establishing itself in the hearts of those who are following the prophetic clock. This is the dispensation of love. Love is receiving renewed emphasis.

We shall proceed to explore the glorious depths of the features of the kind of love that will operate amongst the dwellers on the holy mountain of God. The startling revelations we are about to encounter must urge us to pursue love at its highest level. The love revolution has started in the hearts of thousands of believers around the globe who have keyed into the mind of God. Love is everything because God is love. It is possible to walk in love in spite of the numerous challenges of our times. The love of God is shed abroad in our hearts by the Holy Ghost.

The Atmosphere Of Love

☞ **The wolf shall dwell with the lamb (Isaiah 11:6).**
The wolf is the dread of shepherds. **It is a symbol of deceit and brutality**. Benjamin is described as a wolf because of the warlike nature of the tribe.

> *Benjamin shall ravin as a wolf: in the morning he shall devour the prey, and at night he shall divide the spoil.*
> *Genesis 49:27*

Benjamin ravins like a wolf. The word "ravin" means to pluck off or pull to pieces. Benjamin is portrayed to have the power to devour his prey. The lamb refers to young sheep but originally it included the young of goats. It is a symbol of meekness and innocence. It represents a sacrifice. Jesus Christ is portrayed as the Paschal Lamb. If a lamb dwells in the same place with a wolf, it is in great danger – the wolf will devour it.

The prophet Ezekiel described the sins of Jerusalem by comparing the activities of its leaders with the voracious habits of wolves.

> *Her princes in the midst thereof are like wolves ravening the prey, to shed blood, and to destroy souls, to get dishonest gain.*
>
> *Ezekiel 22:27*

As I mentioned earlier the word ravin means to pluck off or pull to pieces. The leaders of Jerusalem did not love the flock (the lambs). They instead took advantage of them and devoured them and their goods – they pulled them to pieces. These bad leaders fed themselves with the fat and clothed themselves with fleece at the expense of the flock. There is nothing wrong with a pastor or a leader prospering but he must not do so to the detriment of his flock. In the love revolution leaders will discard selfishness and greed. The flock of God will be spared as leaders are motivated by love instead of gain.

We have all heard about wolves in sheep clothing. Wolves are masters in the game of deception. Pretence is their specialty. Jesus hinted that in the last days false prophets with the ravening tendencies of wolves would appear in sheep clothing.

> *Beware of false prophets, which come to you in sheep's clothing, but inwardly they are ravening wolves.*
>
> *Matthew 7:15*

In the prophecy of Isaiah the wolf and the lamb shall dwell together in God's holy mountain. The wolf shall discard its powers of deceit and ravenousness. I see homes of peace without fear and intimidation. Churches are about to step into a dispensation of safety where we can trust our leaders and one another. A new breed of politicians are on the horizon who will not devour nations and their resources.

The wolf shall not hide in its covert only to come out once in a while and devour lambs. It shall dwell or inhabit the same place with the lamb and will not harm the lamb. The wolf will sojourn with the lamb without any arrogance because it knows that the earth is the Lord's and the fullness thereof. To dwell in the holy mountain entails the consciousness that the mountain does not belong to you but to God. The arrogance of the wolf shall depart and the lamb will be safe in this dispensation of love.

Another combination of animals which is used to signal the end of hostilities in the dispensation of love is the leopard and the kid. In ancient times leopards infested the mountains of Syria and made them dreadful. **The leopard is noted for its fierceness and swiftness**. The leopard is smaller than the lion and the tiger but it is swifter than both of them.

> *Their horses also are swifter than the leopards, and are more fierce than the evening wolves: and their horsemen shall spread themselves, and their horsemen shall come from far; they shall fly as the eagle that hasteth to eat.*
> *Habakkuk 1:8*

Leopards do not kill just to satisfy their greed but also to occupy territories. Conquest and occupation are the preserve of leopards.

There are people who are so obsessed with the desire for conquest that they destroy everybody in order to have their way. In the dispensation of love, the leopard will share the same place with the kid. It will be denied its carnivorous

instincts. A new nature will possess the inner being of the leopard to accommodate the kid.

The Bible uses the leopard figuratively to describe many characters. It is used figuratively to describe God in His judgments.

> *Therefore I will be unto them as a lion: as a leopard by the way will I observe them:*
>
> Hosea 13:7

God is portrayed as lying in wait to pounce on backslidden Israel. In the love revolution God will bear His kids in His arms. He will not lie in wait to pounce on them like a leopard.

The leopard is also used figuratively to describe the Macedonian kingdom, which was an oppressive kingdom.

> *After this I beheld, and lo another, like a leopard, which had upon the back of it four wings of a fowl; the beast had also four heads; and dominion was given to it.*
>
> Daniel 7:6

In this dispensation of love controllers and manipulators of power will change their attitudes. The leopard in the Hebrew is *namer* because it is spotted. The Bible mentions the fact that it is impossible in the natural for a leopard to change its spots (Jeremiah 13:23). In the dispensation of love, however, the leopard will be transformed and will lie down with the kid. The leopard will not have to lose its spots before it cohabits with the kid. The change is internal and not external.

In the love revolution we shall maintain our individual characteristics and yet because of love we shall flow together instead of destroying one another. We shall not have to discard our spots to be acceptable.

The kid is a young goat and it is used for food and some scholars believe that it was also used for idolatrous sacrifices. Leopards prey on kids but in this dispensation of love the leopard will lie down with the kid.

People who are impossible to change will receive a circumcision of heart. Some parents are oppressors of their own children. Spouses, bosses and even neighbors may be the oppressors in your life. God promises a dispensation of love where it will be safe for you to lie down with them.

John the revelator had several descriptions of the Antichrist and one of such is the leopard.

> And the beast which I saw was like unto a leopard, and his feet were as the feet of a bear, and his mouth as the mouth of a lion: and the dragon gave him his power, and his seat, and great authority.
>
> *Revelation 13:2*

The Antichrist shall be swift in his operations like the leopard because he has a short time. With magical charm and hypnotizing characteristics the antichrist will seize the hearts of people. Though the antichrist person will not repent as the Scriptures show, some people with the spirit of the antichrist in our time will lose their corrupt tendencies. The leopard shall lie down with the kid. To lie down is a position of rest. One of the activities of the antichrist is to compel people to work for him and worship him. In the new dispensation we shall not be manipulated to work for our taskmasters but we shall lie down with them.

We cannot conclude the issue of the wolf dwelling with the lamb without considering the wonder of how Jesus came into the world as the lamb of God and dwelt amongst sinners and was tempted by the devil. The devil and sinners can be seen as leopards and wolves. Jesus the Lamb of God dwelled amongst us. Love made him dwell among us. He could not be destroyed until He was ready to lay down His life. We must not be afraid to dwell with people who we consider to be dangerous when the Holy Spirit prompts us to do so. Jesus told His disciples that He was sending them as sheep amongst wolves. We are not called to operate amongst angels but men – wolves.

☛ **The calf and the young lion and the fatling together (Isaiah 11:6).**

Isaiah described the unity of the holy mountain dwellers by making reference to the calf, the young lion and the fatling. The calf is the young of the ox species. In Scripture calves are frequently mentioned with respect to their common use in sacrifices. **The lion is regarded as the strongest, most daring and most impressive of all carnivorous animals.** The fatling is the fattened calf – it is an animal fatted for slaughter. It was considered by the Hebrews as the choicest of animal food.

These three animals (the calf, the young lion and the fatling) constitute three different levels of status.

The **calf** and the **young lion** are both young but they are **different kinds** of animals. The difference in classification is the idea here. In spite of the difference in classification between the calf and the young lion they shall operate as a unit in God's holy mountain.

The **calf** and the **fatling** could belong to the same group of animals (fatling could also be used of choice sheep) but they are **different sizes**. The physical appearance of people should not affect the way we receive them or love them. Many spiritual people have been misled by physical appearance.

The **fatling** and the **young lion** are also **different in character** – the fatling is a sacrifice or meat for food and the lion is a carnivorous predator. In the love revolution we should be able to cope with people whose temperaments are different from ours. We must be able to love people and respond to them in such a manner that will lead them to repentance. It is not right to isolate people simply because they don't think the way we think.

The calf and the lion have different origins but the Bible uses the word "together" to link them. "Together" means a unit or alike. In the dispensation of love our skin colour and origin will not hinder the bond of love. Inter-cultural and inter-racial marriages will work. Mixed congregations will work. There is neither male nor female in Christ. The difference between the Greek and the Jew is non consequential. There is no slave or master in Christ. This is one of the amazing features of the love revolution.

> *There is neither Jew nor Greek, there is neither bond nor free, there is neither male nor female: for ye are all one in Christ Jesus.*
>
> *Galatians 3:28*

The oneness of the Body of Christ is the greatest mystery of the Church. Paul devoted his life to instruct the Church to walk in oneness. The walls of partition amongst us must be overthrown. We are not Protestants, Evangelicals or Pentecostals – we are Christians. The recent attempts by Pope Benedict the XVI (born Joseph Alois Ratzinger) to draw the protestant Church of Turkey into talks aimed at bridging the division of over one thousand years between the Catholic Church and Protestants, should tell the spirit filled believer that the time of division is over. I am not calling for ecumenism but the spiritual oneness of the Body of Christ.

> *With all lowliness and meekness, with longsuffering, forbearing one another in love;*

Endeavouring to keep the unity of the Spirit in the bond of peace.

There is one body, and one Spirit, even as ye are called in one hope of your calling;

One Lord, one faith, one baptism,

One God and Father of all, who is above all, and through all, and in you all.

Ephesians 4:2-6

The above emphasis on the oneness of the Body of Christ must find its way back to the Church. We are so divided that the world looks safer than the Church. There is one body, one Spirit, one hope of our calling, one Lord, one faith, one baptism, one God and one Father of all. It is amazing that people with these supernatural factors in common can be so hostile towards one another.

With such elements of oneness given to us by God it is a mystery that we are so divided. The miracle is not that we are one but that we are divided though we have so much in common.

The classification and categorization of people is one of the greatest weaknesses of the modern day Church. Partiality and preferential treatment is meted out to people without shame.

The Bible talks about people having men's persons in admiration because of advantage – they flatter others in order to get favours in return.

*These are murmurers, complainers, walking after their own lusts; and their mouth speaketh great swelling words, **having men's persons in admiration because of advantage.***

Jude 1:16

I have personally struggled in ministry to come to terms with the treatment other preachers and churches meted out to me when I went to speak at their meetings in the early stages of my ministry. They simply looked at my physical structure and I was too slim to earn their respect. Others considered my financial state and because I did not dress a certain kind of way they despised the grace of God on my life. There were others also who used my geographical location in Bolgatanga in northern Ghana to treat me with contempt.

I remember one bad experience I had in a church outside my country. A friend invited me to speak in his church in a distant part of another country. I had to travel five hundred miles from Bolgatanga to Accra in Ghana to catch a plane to the capital city of that country. When I arrived in the city, I took a long flight to the part of the country where my friend was. On arriving at the airport I had to call the leadership of the church to come and fetch me from the airport – they did not know that I was coming to town.

I was driven to a dilapidated building and dumped there – I was to stay there for five days. I almost froze when they informed me that my friend was not in town; he had also not informed the leadership of the church that I was coming. No event had been planned for me. The guesthouse was bad. I could not use the bathroom because it was so small that it was not possible for me to bend down without hitting the walls. Cobwebs stared at me from the roof and the plastic tiles on the floor peeled off without any resistance when I walked on them.

My meals were no better. I believe that the leaders of the church just looked at my slim figure and decided that I was not worthy of any appropriate treatment. I was not one of the big guys they knew – I was not a celebrated preacher. The next day they came to visit me and as we talked they found out that I was a trained pharmacist. As soon as I mentioned that they switched to their native language (a dialect they thought I did not understand) and said that "this man is a big man and we should not have accommodated him here." They came back to me in the English language and said that they had made a mistake in bringing me to that guesthouse. They said that they had actually arranged a better place for me but there was a mix up. They promised to come and fetch me to a better place later in the day.

My friends did not know that I speak some amount of the native language they spoke – I had heard the actual reason why they brought me to the bad guesthouse. The reason was that they did not know that I was a trained pharmacist. If they had known this they would have treated me better. Such is the wrong philosophy of our world. When they got up to leave I bade them good-bye in the native language they had spoken and they were startled. They asked me whether I spoke the language and I answered in the affirmative. The embarrassment on their faces was enough to paralyze them.

Their shock was further heightened when the following day, during the Sunday morning the Lord used me powerfully to deliver the Word of God. There was an amazing manifestation of the word of knowledge and miracles of healing and deliverance. The senior associate pastor with other leaders who had told me that they could only consider if I could speak on Sunday morning suddenly wanted me to speak for another three days. I turned down the invitation and headed back to Ghana the following day. It was obvious from the actions of my hosts that they just wanted to use and abuse the grace of God on my life. I did not matter to them as a person.

My outward appearance and country of origin was not enough to impress my hosts. They did not have enough "philadelphia" to entertain strangers. They might have constructed their own way of categorizing and classifying people and initially I did not fit into their way of thinking. In the love revolution the calf and the young lion shall dwell together as a unit. We must learn to see ourselves as being alike.

161

Couples with different temperaments should be able to enjoy their marriage. Differences in opinion and criticism of one another should be accommodated with love in the house of God. A pastor should not fire people from his board simply because they disagree with him. Members must not storm out of a church because the pastor did not listen to their advice. It is possible for pastors to work together in spite of their differences on petty doctrinal issues. Selfish ambition has resulted in too many church splits and divorces because people want to have their own way in everything.

The calf, the young lion and the fatling shall be led by a little child. They shall co-operate with one another so much so that even a little child can lead them without difficulty. Humility is a central feature of the dispensation of love. God's people will submit to the leadership of anyone God elects to lead them even if the person is a child.

In the dispensation of love no one is too big to be led and no one is too small to lead.

Shepherds will have all manner of people in their sheepfold and they are supposed to love them and lead them together. Though diverse in our constitutions we must be able to exist and operate as a single unit. Leaders must develop their skills and cultivate enough love to lead the calf, the young lion and the fatling together.

And the cow and the bear shall feed (Isaiah 11:7).

The cow and the bear shall feed, their young ones shall lie down together and the lion shall eat straw like the ox. The idea of the cow and bear feeding is similar to the mystery of the wolf and the lamb dwelling together.

Herbivorous bears live in caves in high and rugged mountains and come out especially at night to feed on roots and vegetables.

Figuratively, the bear is known for its ferocious nature, especially when the she bear is robbed of her whelps (Hosea 13:8). Various species of bears are classified as carnivores, omnivores, herbivores or insectivores. I believe that Isaiah 11:7 refers to carnivorous bears like the one that attempted to attack the sheep of David and the two which attacked and killed forty two children for mocking Elisha. The reason is that Isaiah had a miracle in mind when he talked about the cow and the bear feeding – the miracle of a bear not feasting on a cow. Cows feed on plants and it will be no miracle for a herbivorous bear or omnivorous bear to feed with the cow. The prophet is definitely talking about a carnivorous bear that feeds on animals and would rather feed on a cow than feed with the cow.

In the dispensation of love we shall not devour one another – the cow and the bear shall feed and the lion will eat straw like the ox. The lion will not feel too big to eat what the ox eats. This means all of us will be able to condescend to men of low estate. Spiritual pride will not isolate us from fellowship with other believers we consider to be inferior to us.

A major revelation in Isaiah 11:7 is that the young ones of the cow and the bear shall lie together. When the young bear and the young cow see their older ones feeding together, they will also flow together. The signals are clear – a generation of love people are coming up who will not allow the seed of bitterness and enmity to pass on to them from previous generations.

Nations are at war because of inherited conflicts. Conflicts which took place hundreds of years ago are still having their toll on our generation. It is rather unfortunate that we have allowed these conflicts to divide us and we are also busy creating new ones for the next generation. It is common to find parents insisting that their children should have nothing to do with their cousins because the parents are at war with their brothers and cousins. Aunties are zealously transferring war-mongering spirits to their children. The young ones of the bear and the cow shall feed together because the older ones have set a good example.

Barriers are going up everywhere with pastors threatening their members with curses if they fellowship in other churches. There is a strong need for a defiant generation – one that would refuse to inherit a war-mongering spirit.

Jesus, the lion of the tribe of Judah humbled Himself and came into the world. He shared this world with us – he ate what we eat and slept where we sleep. His love for humanity was proved beyond all reasonable doubt. He carried His humanity so strongly that His deity was not abused. We must learn from Jesus by humbling ourselves when the situation calls for it. Our privileges must not make it impossible for us to come down to the level of the people we are called to minister to.

Age long traditions are denying good people the opportunity to marry one another. A few years ago we had an interesting case in our church. A brother wanted to marry a sister only to be told that it was a taboo to do so. The reason the elders of the respective ethnic groups gave was that a conflict occurred between their two ethnic groups over one hundred years ago. The story has it that a man from one of the villages impregnated a woman from the other one. In the process of time he became wicked towards her and murdered her with the pregnancy. The aggrieved ethnic group then vowed that they would no more have any marital unions with the other group. It was a taboo for any woman from their village to marry from the other village.

When the brother and sister from our church declared their intentions to marry they came face to face with this taboo. It is still believed that it is forbidden for people from the two traditional areas to marry. The matter was brought before me and I decided that if they loved each other and it was the will of God for them to marry, nothing should stop them. With my endorsement of their convictions they went ahead with the marriage and we blessed them. It has been some years now since they married and their union is blessed with two children. Their marriage is a happy one and there is no curse in it.

This couple defied the taboo. They refused to allow their born again lives to be hindered by the traditions of unregenerate people. If the older bear and older cow refuse to feed together their younger ones must refuse to follow their example. There are certain cases where some people wickedly set themselves against people we love. They formulate plans to destroy them and erode their gains. In such cases we must stand for justice and not compromise with the evildoers by fellowshipping with them.

I cannot leave this subject without stressing that love should not compromise the principles of loyalty, patriotism and the spirit of nationalism. We cannot forge alliances with avowed enemies of our leaders, churches, families and nations in the name of love. Under circumstances like that if we betray the trust of the people who love us, we are not walking in love. We must look at things objectively when there is a problem between those we owe allegiance to and others. If we judge them to have been wrongly treated we must stand by them and refuse to keep company with those that want to destroy our loved ones. This does not mean that we should make offending people our enemies but we have to walk in wisdom not to inflict more wounds on our own people.

It is very common for people who want to hurt your loved ones to use you as a weapon to fight against them. They pretend to love you but in actual fact they are using you as a weapon to fight back at their enemies.

🏴 **The sucking child shall play on the hole of the asp (Isaiah 11:8).**

The sucking child shall play on the hole of the asp, and the weaned child shall put his hand on the cockatrice's den. **The asp is the Egyptian cobra. It is a small and very poisonous serpent which loves to live in holes. The cockatrice is a horned viper which is also a poisonous serpent of about one foot in length.** The idea here is that in the dispensation of love the nursing child will play at the hole of the cobra and the weaned child will put his hand on the viper's den – children will play with deadly snakes.

A number of things run through my mind when I consider the child playing on the holes of snakes. This pictorial depiction of love in the holy mountain of God presents very interesting features of the love revolution.

Firstly, there is the issue of **invasion**. Invasion is going into another person's territory. We see children invading serpents' holes. True love permits a certain degree of the invasion of privacy. Adam and Eve were naked and they were not ashamed. It is inappropriate for married couples and brethren to have too many things they hide from one another. There are couples who are not permitted to see each other's financial situations. They don't know where each one goes neither are they accountable to each other. As much as we are individuals true love is not afraid to allow others into its privacy.

Secondly, **innocence** is portrayed in the child playing on the hole of serpents. By innocence I don't mean ignorance. I am referring to the lack of experience that makes you trust people. Children ˡᵒⁿ't take stock of the wrongs of the past and allow them to hinder ·ⁿ towards others. Love does not keep record of wrong ·ᵗ not be wise in our own conceit. When people are ᵉk to protect themselves from others at all cost ⎦ true love.

The third thing that comes to mind is **intimacy**. The child puts his hand in the hole of the snake. They share a common hole and come very close to each other without the fear of being hurt. Close personal relationships should be sought with all diligence. It is imperative for intimate relationships to be cultivated amongst God's people. There are many relationships around us but they are very shallow. We cannot share our innermost feelings, fears and thoughts with anybody for the fear of being abused. In the love revolution children will play on the hole of snakes.

Innovation is the fourth issue that comes up. Innovation is the use of new ideas to achieve a goal. Love allows innovative ventures amongst God's people. The fear of mistakes and the attendant retribution are completely eradicated in the love revolution. The move of God in our time is so strong that people are moving forward without any limits. The tendency of people to make mistakes rises with the thousands of attempts they make to let things happen. In the love revolution the child takes time off playing with his normal friends and looks for new friends in snakes. The child leaves familiar territory and explores the holes of snakes. In an atmosphere of love where people know that they will not be crucified for their mistakes, adventure and innovation are promoted.

The fifth idea in the child playing at the hole of poisonous snakes is **indulgence**. The word indulgence can be used in the negative sense but in the harmless sense it can be used to mean something enjoyable which we do for pleasure. In the dispensation of love children will indulge in the pleasure of playing on the holes of deadly snakes. Children will have fun with snakes. Our assemblies and fellowships should not be too stifling. Where the Spirit of the Lord is there is liberty. The kingdom of God is not in the strict observation of touch not, taste not and handle not.

Wherefore if ye be dead with Christ from the rudiments of the world, why, as though living in the world, are ye subject to ordinances,
(Touch not; taste not; handle not;
Colossians 2:20-21

The kingdom of God is not governed by what to eat and what not to eat – a strict adherence to Jewish laws. Condemnation of people based on man-made religious laws is not the feature of the love revolution.

For the kingdom of God is not meat and drink; but righteousness, and peace, and joy in the Holy Ghost.
Romans 14:17

Lustful entertainment is not to be encouraged in the house of God. Nevertheless, righteousness must flow with peace and joy in the Holy Ghost.

In the dispensation of love there is fullness of joy. People find excitement in one another. The atmosphere is electrified with liberty and joy as people share everything with one another. Such was the atmosphere when the first century church was born.

And they, continuing daily with one accord in the temple, and breaking bread from house to house, did eat their meat with gladness and singleness of heart,
Praising God, and having favour with all the people. And the Lord added to the church daily such as should be saved.
Acts 2:46-47

The apostles broke bread from house to house – they invaded one another's privacy. They also ate their meat with gladness and singleness of heart. This is what church should look like. This must be the atmosphere in our homes. The fear of being hurt by someone is not healthy for the Church. Dangerous people must change their characteristics and those that live in constant fear must discard their fears.

☞ They shall not hurt nor destroy in all my holy mountain (Isaiah 11:9).

The animals in the holy mountain of God shall not hurt nor destroy one another. This is the summary of everything we have said above. The condition of perfect tranquility will precede the explosion of the knowledge of the Lord in the holy mountain of God. The ultimate will of God is for His knowledge to cover the earth as the waters cover the sea. This knowledge is not impotent knowledge. It is translated into the power to perform.

Paul connected the knowledge of the Lord with the flow of His power.

> *That I may know him, and the power of his resurrection, and the fellowship of his sufferings, being made conformable unto his death;*
>
> *Philippians 3:10*

The knowledge of Christ releases the power of His resurrection in us. There is a great need for the manifestation of resurrection power in the Church. We have operated below the capacity God wants us to. The reason for this dismal operation in the power of God is our lack of knowledge of the Lord. We don't know God well enough to flow in His power.

Daniel's prophecy also elucidates the fact that power and knowledge are connected.

> *And such as do wickedly against the covenant shall he corrupt by flatteries: but the people that do know their*

God shall be strong, and do exploits.
Daniel 11:32

Daniel says that the people who know their God shall be strong and do exploits. The ability to do exploits lies in the knowledge of God. This generation has a strong desire to do exploits but we are yet to come to terms with the fact that the knowledge of God is the key. We have emphasized self-awareness and self-worth so much that it is not about God anymore. In our attempt to discover who we are we have thrown who God is out of the window. The fact of the matter is that there are not many people who can teach us and stir us up to know God, because few people really know God.

When we take the connection between the knowledge of God and power into consideration, the words of Isaiah in Isaiah 11:9 become clearer. Isaiah said that the inhabitants of the holy mountain shall not hurt nor destroy one another and then the earth shall be full of the knowledge of the Lord as the waters cover the sea.

If we combine all these things we have a sequence like:
- **The people shall not hurt nor destroy one another in God's holy mountain.**
- **The harmonious atmosphere in the holy mountain leads to the knowledge of the Lord.**
- **The knowledge of God releases the power of God throughout the earth as the waters cover the sea.**

There is no doubt that our generation is seeking the manifestation of God's power on earth. We see people everywhere in conferences, crusades and other spiritual events in search of the miraculous touch of God. As I draw the curtains on this book it is important for me to reiterate that love is everything. If we love one another we shall not hurt nor destroy one another. This demonstration of "philadelphia" is a great factor in the release of the power of God.

We have applied various principles to key into the power of God and His resources to no avail. Traces of power and glimpses of glory have been experienced here and there but that is not enough. The principles and even the rigorous spiritual disciplines like fasting and prayer we have employed have not achieved the best results for the kingdom of God and us. We must go back to the more excellent way – the way of love. We have walked in selfishness and hatred for so long that it will only take a revolution to bring love back to the Church. The assurance is that there is a move of the Holy Spirit on earth that is carrying the love revolution anywhere God's people are willing to embrace it.

Love is everything because God is love. Love is the best tool we can employ for conquest; all other tools are manipulative and with time they tend to backfire – they that take the sword shall die by the sword. It is only the labour of love that pleases God. It is futile to engage in labour without love because it profits us nothing. Our faith operates by love. Without love faith will cease to operate and the end result will be that there shall be no accomplishments. Seeing that faith is so crucial to our triumphal Christian living we must do our best to feed our faith with love so that it will grow.

Jesus is known for His love. His love is His greatest virtue. He loved us to the end by sacrificing His life on the cross for us. Love drove Him to give us everything He had including His life. There is no greater love than this – that a man should lay down His life for His friends.

The prophet Isaiah painted an excellent picture of the life of Jesus as the Lamb of God in Isaiah 53. In this scripture he showed how Jesus loved us unto death. He also gave a detailed picture of the suffering Jesus took upon Himself for our sakes.

> *Surely he hath borne our griefs, and carried our sorrows: yet we did esteem him stricken, smitten of God, and afflicted.*

But he was wounded for our transgressions, he was bruised for our iniquities: the chastisement of our peace was upon him; and with his stripes we are healed.

All we like sheep have gone astray; we have turned every one to his own way; and the LORD hath laid on him the iniquity of us all.

He was oppressed, and he was afflicted, yet he opened not his mouth: he is brought as a lamb to the slaughter, and as a sheep before her shearers is dumb, so he openeth not his mouth.

He was taken from prison and from judgment: and who shall declare his generation? for he was cut off out of the land of the living: for the transgression of my people was he stricken.

And he made his grave with the wicked, and with the rich in his death; because he had done no violence, neither was any deceit in his mouth.

Isaiah 53:4-9

This is what love is all about. Jesus bore our griefs and carried our sorrows. The chastisement of our peace was upon Him. He was wounded for our transgressions and bruised for our iniquities. The Lamb of God was oppressed and afflicted but for our sakes He did not open His mouth. Jesus was led to the slaughter and for our sakes He died the most shameful death. He was stricken for the transgression of His people and made His grave with the wicked. The love revolution seeks to entrench this kind of love amongst God's people. We must not love less than He did.

May I borrow the words of the author of Hebrews to remind you to **let brotherly love continue**. Resist every temptation to walk in darkness. Don't stop loving. Seek the purest form of love – unfeigned love. THE LOVE REVOLUTION HAS BEGUN; EMBRACE IT.

LET US PRAY:

God of love and peace I pray in the name of Jesus FOR YOUR EMPOWERMENT. I ask that you shed your love abroad in my heart by the Holy Spirit. Deliver me from the spirit of hatred and the bondage of bitterness. I plead with you for the spirit of love to penetrate the darkness of my heart. Transform my heart and let it be adapted to contain the love of God. Eternal Father and God of supernatural love empower me to walk in love and let me endeavor to maintain the bond of peace in the Body of Christ.

I dedicate myself to brotherly love. Reveal your nature to me and make me a partaker of the eternal nature of love. Unite me with your essence and let me live in you. Dear Father, touch me that I may touch the world. Nothing short of a revolution will precipitate the love of God in my heart. Your people are surrounded by so many forces of hatred and selfishness, that only you can deliver us from being destroyed.

We confess that our love for you and other people has gone cold. We confess that we have placed our achievements above our love for people. Forgive us for sacrificing others to get what we want.
Let there be love.
Let there be light.
Let there be life.

Almighty and Eternal God empower me to love you before I serve you. Give me the grace to love others before I minister to them. I thank you for loving me. The greatest gift you have ever given me is your love and I am forever grateful. I ask you, Father, to bless me with a heart of love and an environment of peace and glorious tranquility.

I thank you God of love and grace for revealing the mystery of eternal love to us. Through this operation of love you have made us more than conquerors. Blessed be the LORD forever and ever, AMEN.